THE
NO TIME
TO COOK
BOOK

THE
NO TIME
TO COOK
BOOK

100 modern, simple recipes in 20 minutes or less

LAURA HERRING

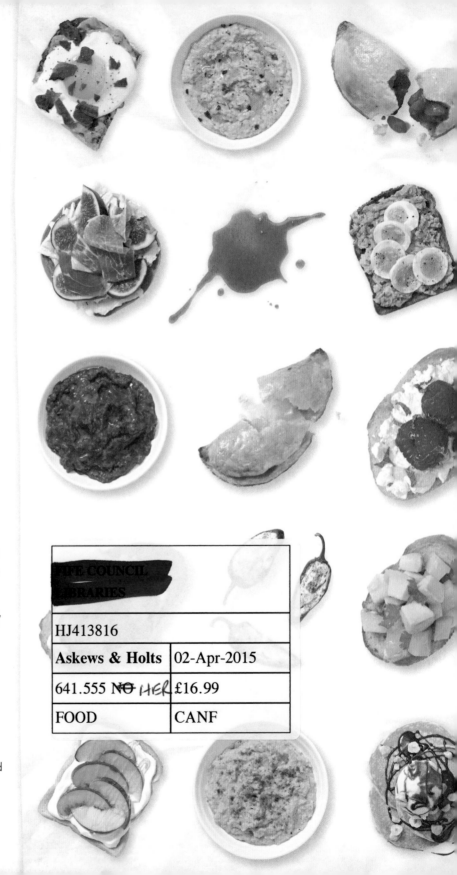

Senior Editor Bob Bridle
Designer Harriet Yeomans
Editorial Assistant Alice Kewellhampton
Design Assistant Laura Buscemi
Managing Editor Dawn Henderson
Managing Art Editor Christine Keilty
Senior Jacket Creative Nicola Powling
Jacket Art Editor Kathryn Wilding
Pre-Production Producer Andy Hilliard
Senior Producer Jen Scothern
Deputy Art Director Maxine Pedliham
Art Director Peter Luff
Publisher Peggy Vance

Additional contributor
Elena Rosemond-Hoerr

Studio photography
Stuart West and William Reavell

First published in Great Britain in 2015
by Dorling Kindersley Limited
80 Strand, London, WC2R 0RL

Copyright © 2015
Dorling Kindersley Limited
A Penguin Random House Company
10 9 8 7 6 5 4 3 2 1
001–259427–Apr/2015

A CIP catalogue record for this book
is available from the British Library
ISBN: 978–0–2411–8637–4

Colour reproduction by AltaImage
Printed and bound in China

All images © Dorling Kindersley Limited
For further information see:
www.dkimages.com

A WORLD OF IDEAS:
SEE ALL THERE IS TO KNOW

CONTENTS

FOREWORD

The No Time to Cook Book is packed with hundreds of tempting recipes, inspiring ideas, and ingenious time-saving tips for cooks in a hurry. Forget takeaways and ready meals, we aim to show you that fast cooking can be easy, enjoyable, and – most importantly – delicious.

I love cooking. Nothing gives me more pleasure than pottering about in the kitchen for hours on end. But really, who has time for that? More often than not I find myself hastily assembling a meal somewhere between fridge and plate, or grabbing something on my way out of the door. However, I still want to eat nutritious, tasty, and exciting food – which is where *The No Time to Cook Book* comes in.

The recipes in this book are all designed with the time-pressed cook in mind. "Plan-of-action" panels present the key stages at a glance, so you'll never get lost in a complicated method again. Step-by-step illustrations show you what you should be doing and when. Special features demonstrate how to mix-and-match flavours depending on your preference (and what's in your cupboard), and innovative info-graphics put the fun back into cooking, even when you're low on time.

In the first section there are practical ideas for getting set up for quick cooking. You'll find out what equipment you really need, which ingredients to stock up on, and how to prepare some key ingredients quickly and efficiently. We also share some of the best time-saving tips around.

The sections that follow group recipes into mealtimes, so you can quickly flip to the recipes you need. Choose from speedy breakfast and brunch ideas, lunches that can be whipped up in no time (and many of them packed up and eaten on the go), amazing mid-week dinners, and – my personal favourite – a fantastic selection of starters, sharing platters, and main dishes for when you have people over and little time to prepare. Finally, as no meal is complete without something sweet, there are many moreish ideas for puddings and treats, too.

Flavour is key, and all the recipes use fresh, modern ingredients from cuisines around the world. In 20 minutes or less you can visit the Middle East via a warming shakshouka, taste fiery Dan Dan Noodles from Thailand's street vendors, enjoy heady Mediterranean flavours in a Feta, Tomato, and Red Pesto Tart, or jet over to Latin America for some speedy ceviche. There are grills, pies, pastas, soups, salads, stews, cookies, chocolate puddings, and much, much more. So whatever you feel like eating, whatever the time of day – even when you definitely have "no time to cook" – you'll find that the perfect quick recipe is just waiting for you here!

Laura

THE QUICK
KITCHEN

ESSENTIAL EQUIPMENT

Investing in a few basic pieces of kitchen equipment will mean you always have the right tool for the job. This will save you time when preparing and cooking your food, and make spending time in the kitchen a pleasure.

It's also important to organize your equipment and ingredients (see pp12–15) so that you always know where to find things – your time is best spent making delicious food, not hunting for an elusive frying pan or jar of mayonnaise!

Keep your saucepans stacked by size, your utensils in easy reach, and your cupboards, fridge, and freezer tidily stocked. Turn cans and jars so that the labels are facing outwards and clearly visible, and when labelling your own food be sure to use permanent marker, which won't rub off.

WOODEN SPOON
A trusty wooden spoon, for stirring and beating, is durable and won't scratch your pots and pans.

FRYING PAN
Buy one that is large enough to cook an omelette. A frying pan with a lid is helpful to speed up cooking.

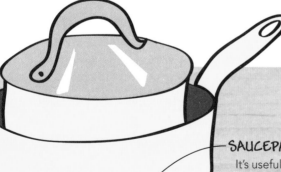

SAUCEPANS (WITH LIDS)
It's useful to have a range of pans to hand, including a large stockpot, a mid-sized pan for cooking pasta and potatoes, and a small pan for sauces.

SHARP KNIVES
Use large knives (top) for slicing vegetables and meat, and a smaller knife (bottom) for peeling and coring fruit and finely chopping vegetables.

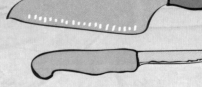

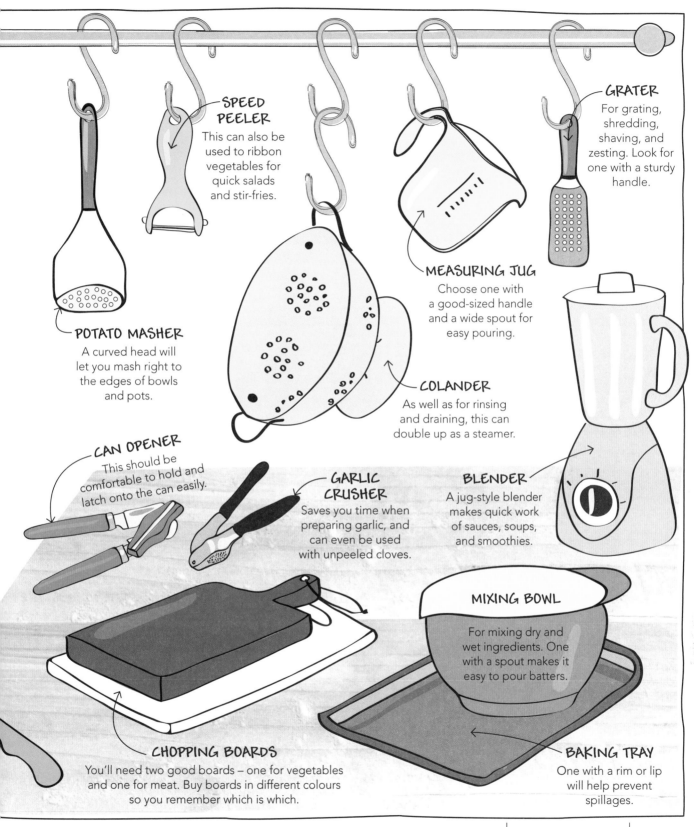

SPEED PEELER
This can also be used to ribbon vegetables for quick salads and stir-fries.

GRATER
For grating, shredding, shaving, and zesting. Look for one with a sturdy handle.

POTATO MASHER
A curved head will let you mash right to the edges of bowls and pots.

MEASURING JUG
Choose one with a good-sized handle and a wide spout for easy pouring.

COLANDER
As well as for rinsing and draining, this can double up as a steamer.

CAN OPENER
This should be comfortable to hold and latch onto the can easily.

GARLIC CRUSHER
Saves you time when preparing garlic, and can even be used with unpeeled cloves.

BLENDER
A jug-style blender makes quick work of sauces, soups, and smoothies.

MIXING BOWL
For mixing dry and wet ingredients. One with a spout makes it easy to pour batters.

CHOPPING BOARDS
You'll need two good boards – one for vegetables and one for meat. Buy boards in different colours so you remember which is which.

BAKING TRAY
One with a rim or lip will help prevent spillages.

SMART SHOPPING

Aim to do a big shop every couple of weeks to replenish your store-cupboard ingredients, then stock up on fresh items in between. This will allow you to produce quick, delicious meals using the core ingredients on your shelves. See below for key store-cupboard ingredients and pages 14–15 for your fridge and freezer essentials.

STORE-CUPBOARD ESSENTIALS

CANS
- **Chopped tomatoes** – for quick pasta sauces and to bulk up leftovers.
- **Beans** (such as cannellini, kidney, and borlotti) – add to soups and stews for extra texture, fibre, and protein.
- **Chickpeas** – add to salads, stews, and curries, or turn into hummus.
- **Coconut milk** – use in noodle soups and curries.
- **Salmon, tuna, and crab** – use in pasta sauces, salads, wraps, tarts, and fishcakes.
- **Fruit** (such as peaches or pineapple pieces) – for smoothies, tarts, and pies.

JARS
- **Sun-dried tomatoes**, artichoke pieces, and roasted peppers – use on pizzas, in salads, and as part of a mezze.
- **Pesto** – use as a pasta sauce, to add flavour to dressings, and mixed through mayo as a dip or spread.

DRIED GOODS
- **Pasta** – the ultimate quick-cook standby.
- **Rice noodles** – use in soups, stir-fries, and salads.
- **Quick-cook rice** – as a side and in risottos and salads.
- **Bulgur wheat** – as a side or in a salad.
- **Couscous** – as a side for curries and stews, or use in salads.
- **Oats** – for porridge, muesli, and granola; or use in flapjacks and cookies.
- **Plain flour** – for pastries, cookies, cakes, and quick white sauces.
- **Sugar** – add a teaspoon to tomato sauce for extra flavour.
- **Good-quality stock cubes** – as a base for soups and to add flavour to stews.
- **Mixed nuts and dried fruits** – to top oats and yogurt, or to use in cookie dough, salads, and curries.
- **Wraps and tortillas** – for fajitas, lunch wraps, and as a quick pizza base.

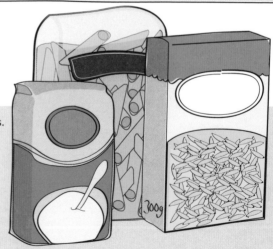

SAUCES AND PASTES

- **Harissa** – use in sauces and with meatballs, or mix with mayo as a dip.
- **Tomato purée** – add to tomato sauces for richness.
- **Mayonnaise** – flavour with herbs, harissa, or lemon juice for dressings; mix with garlic, pesto, or harissa as a dip or spread.
- **Worcestershire sauce** – add to meat-based dishes for extra flavour; sprinkle over cheese on toast.
- **Tabasco sauce** – add a few drops for instant heat.
- **Soy sauce** – use in stir-fries, noodle soups, and as a dip.
- **Good-quality curry paste** – for quick curries, and to spread over meat and fish as an instant marinade.

ON YOUR WINDOW SILL

Fresh, growing herbs – such as parsley, basil, mint, and thyme – add flavour during cooking, and are perfect as a garnish, torn into salads, or as part of a filling for sandwiches and wraps.

OILS AND VINEGARS

- **Olive oil** – for general cooking.
- **Extra-virgin olive oil** – for dressings and dips, and for drizzling.
- **Vegetable or sunflower oil** – for frying at high temperatures.
- **Balsamic vinegar** – for dressings and dips, and for adding sweetness to tomato sauces.
- **Red or white wine vinegar** – add to stews, soups, and sauces to elevate the flavours.

DRIED HERBS AND SPICES

- **Chilli flakes** – sprinkle over soups and use in stews and sauces.
- **Bay leaves** – add to rice and stews for extra flavour.
- **Ground cinnamon** – sprinkle over breakfast oats, add to stews, and use in cookies and cakes.
- **Cayenne pepper** – use as a spicier, warmer alternative to black pepper.
- **Ground coriander** – add to curries and tomato sauces.
- **Ground ginger** – add to curries and sauces; use instead of fresh ginger in stir-fries.

- **Mixed Italian herbs** – use in sauces or scatter over fish or chicken before cooking.
- **Salt and black peppercorns** – for seasoning most dishes.

Good buys
Look out for ingredients that will save you precious minutes, such as quick-cook rice, fresh pasta, and even pre-washed salads.

CONTINUED

IN THE FRIDGE

FRESH SALAD AND GREEN VEG

Use in main-meal salads and side salads, add to stir-fries, or serve alongside simply cooked meat or fish.

EGGS

Endlessly versatile for quick cooking.

YOGURT

Serve with berries and oats for an instant breakfast, add to smoothies, or use as an accompaniment to spicy foods. Thin down and flavour with pesto, harissa, or lemon juice to use as a dressing.

IN THE FREEZER

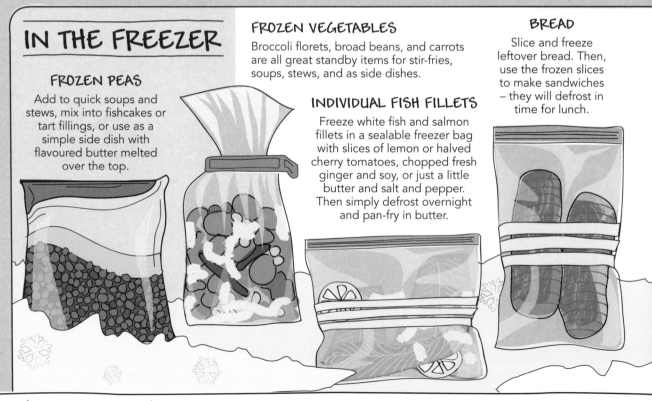

FROZEN PEAS

Add to quick soups and stews, mix into fishcakes or tart fillings, or use as a simple side dish with flavoured butter melted over the top.

FROZEN VEGETABLES

Broccoli florets, broad beans, and carrots are all great standby items for stir-fries, soups, stews, and as side dishes.

INDIVIDUAL FISH FILLETS

Freeze white fish and salmon fillets in a sealable freezer bag with slices of lemon or halved cherry tomatoes, chopped fresh ginger and soy, or just a little butter and salt and pepper. Then simply defrost overnight and pan-fry in butter.

BREAD

Slice and freeze leftover bread. Then, use the frozen slices to make sandwiches – they will defrost in time for lunch.

MUSTARD
Spread over steaks before cooking, combine with olive oil to make a quick dressing, or mix with mayo and use in sandwiches and salads.

OLIVES
Add to salads and sauces, use as a topping for pizzas, and include as part of a mezze.

BUTTER
For general cooking and to add richness to risottos. Also, flavour with herbs, garlic, or chilli flakes and melt over steaks, rice, or cooked vegetables.

BACON
Chop and cook with onions as the base for a tomato sauce, or fry until crispy and scatter over salads for a quick flavour hit.

Bulk-buy deals
Take advantage of any bulk-buy deals or price reductions on multi-packs. You may not need several packets of minced beef or chicken breasts now, but freeze them individually and you'll be set for several meals to come.

CHICKEN PORTIONS
Chicken breasts, thighs, and drumsticks are extremely versatile and quick to cook. (Always make sure they are thoroughly defrosted before cooking.)

STOCK
Use as the base for soups, noodle broths, and to add flavour to stews or when cooking rice or couscous.

MINCED MEAT
Use for meatballs, burgers, and quick pasta sauces.

MIXED BERRIES
Use in smoothies, with breakfast oats and yogurt, or in desserts.

READY-TO-ROLL PUFF PASTRY
Perfect for making quick pies and tarts.

SPEEDY SKILLS MASTERCLASS

DICING AN ONION

1 Chop off each end of the onion – the root and tip.

2 Rest a flat end on the chopping board and cut the onion in half.

3 Peel off the skin of one half and rest the flat side on the board with the cut ends facing left and right in front of you.

PREPARING A PEPPER

1 Slice off the top and bottom of the pepper.

2 Pull out the seeds and white membrane.

3 Cut the pepper in half from top to bottom.

PREPARING AN AVOCADO

1 Carefully slice all the way around the avocado through to the stone.

2 Holding the avocado in the palm of your hand, use your other hand to twist the top half of the avocado to separate the halves.

CHOPPING HERBS

1 Strip the leaves from the stems and gather them in a tight pile.

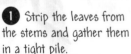

2 Slice through the herbs, holding them together with your other hand.

CHOPPING GARLIC

1 Use the flat edge of a large knife blade and pound the garlic clove, pressing down with your palm.

You may not be able to chop vegetables as fast as a professional chef (who has, after all, been practising for years), but here are some top tips to help you on your way. Use a sharp knife and start off slowly until you gain in confidence.

4 Slice along the length of the onion, holding it in place with your fingers.

5 Pile a few slices on top of each other and, holding them in place with your fingers, slice in line with the straight edge. The layers of the onion will help produce neat cubes.

6 Finish with a few extra chops so the pieces are even. Repeat with the rest of the slices and the other onion half.

4 Open out one half and either pull off or cut out any remaining seeds and ribs.

5 Holding the pepper open, slice along its length to create batons.

6 For dice, hold the batons firmly together and slice crossways. Repeat with the other pepper half.

3 Use the blade of a sharp knife to twist and remove the avocado stone.

4 Use a butter knife to carefully slice along the inside of the flesh. For dice, slice crossways, too.

5 Use a spoon to scoop out the flesh. Repeat with the other avocado half.

2 Discard the skin and slice into slivers lengthways, then cut across into tiny chunks.

PREPARING CHILLI

1 Cut in half lengthways, then scrape out the seeds and remove the stem.

2 Slice each half lengthways into strips. For dice, hold the strips firmly together and slice crossways.

20 TIME-SAVING TIPS

① FLAVOUR HITS

Add instant flavour with some simple ingredients. A squeeze of lemon juice, scattering of zest, splash of chilli sauce, or some freshly chopped herbs all add lots of flavour with very little effort.

② SCRUB UP

When you come home from food shopping, wash fresh produce before putting it away. That way you won't have to scrub it clean when you're pressed for time making dinner.

③ THE NIGHT BEFORE...

Take meat or fish out of the freezer and let it defrost in the fridge overnight. Also, check that you have everything you need – you can pick up any last-minute items on your way home from work the next day.

④ FREEZER MARINADES

Combine pieces of meat with marinade ingredients (see pp198–9), seal in a plastic bag, then pop them in the freezer. When you defrost the meat, it will be flavoured and ready to cook.

⑤ FLAVOURED BUTTERS

Finely chop leftover herbs, mix with softened butter, and freeze. You can then slice off rounds and use while cooking for a herby flavour hit (add to the pan when frying steak, melt over vegetables or rice, or toss through fresh pasta).

⑥ WAYS WITH ICE-CUBE TRAYS

Freeze any leftover wine in an ice-cube tray. This saves you having to open a fresh bottle just to add a splash when cooking. You can also freeze cubes of stock and fresh herbs in olive oil for instant flavour.

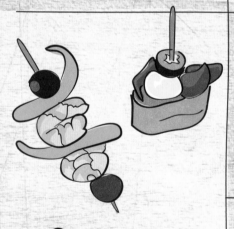

⑦ IT'S A BREEZE IF YOU FREEZE

Make a big batch of your favourite meal and freeze leftovers in individual portions. That way you'll have dinner ready at a moment's notice. You can do the same for pudding – just make individual desserts in ramekins, and freeze.

⑧ LITTLE HELPERS

Many cooks spoil the broth... but a helping hand goes a long way! Why not enlist a friendly sous chef to chop, stir, and help clean up as you go along?

⑨ INSTANT SNACKS

Worried that there is nothing for your guests to nibble on? Simply skewer a selection of olives, anchovies, cheeses, hams, cherry tomatoes, sun-dried peppers – or any other tasty morsels you have in the store-cupboard or fridge!

⑩ GET TO KNOW YOUR RECIPE

Read the recipe all the way through before you start. Knowing exactly what you need to do, and the right order to do it in, will save you time and avoid any surprises once you get going.

⑪ BE FLEXIBLE

Don't worry if you haven't got a particular ingredient. Rather than spending time looking for an alternative recipe, just swap the ingredient for something similar.

Here are our top 20 tips for the time-pressed cook. There's advice about ways of getting ahead before you start, tricks for cutting down the time you spend preparing and cooking your food, ingenious ways to add instant flavour and interest to your meals, and much more besides.

12 BE PREPARED

Weigh, measure, and prep your ingredients first. This will prevent any delays when you suddenly have to juice a lemon or deseed a chilli, say, when you're meant to be stirring a sauce.

13 COOK ONCE, EAT TWICE

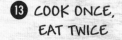

Once you're in the kitchen, apron on, it doesn't take much extra effort to prepare two dishes at the same time. While your oven is heating up tonight's pork chops, why not pop in a couple of chicken breasts on a separate tray? You will save money on your energy bill and be well on the way to tomorrow's dinner.

14 CHOP, CHOP!

Don't just chop one onion, chop two while you're at it! Then, freeze the second one in a sealed freezer bag for another time (the same applies to most chopped veg and herbs). When you're ready to use it, just tip the frozen veg straight into the pan.

15 SIZE MATTERS

Chop your meat or veg into small pieces to reduce the cooking time. Equally, thinner-cut steaks, or thicker pieces of meat that have been flattened, will cook very quickly.

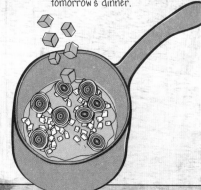

16 COOKING METHODS

Pan-frying, griddling, grilling, and stir-frying are much quicker than baking in the oven or slowly simmering on the hob. Lean cuts of meat and leafy vegetables, for example, only require a quick pan-fry or steam.

17 YOUR FAVOURITE CUP

Rather than weighing out rice, pasta, or other dried goods each time, find a cup or mug that holds the perfect portion size and use that instead. Also, learn to recognize what a tablespoon of oil looks like in the pan so you can simply swirl it in.

18 GET STARTED

Before you do anything else, boil the kettle and turn on the oven (if needed). As soon as the recipe calls for boiling water or for something to be popped in the oven, you'll be ready to go in an instant.

20 KEEP IT CLEAN

Cooking a meal in 20 minutes is fantastic; spending the next hour cleaning up, less so! As you go along, put any waste in the bin, rinse the chopping board, and wipe the worktop. That way you'll just be left with a small amount of washing up.

19 DON'T PLATE UP

Save time when serving by placing large sharing platters in the middle of the table. It's quicker than plating up individual portions and creates a relaxed, sharing atmosphere.

SPEEDY BREAKFAST
AND BRUNCH

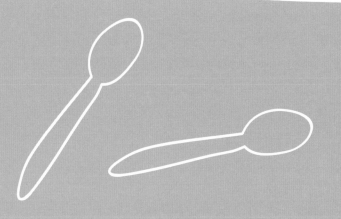

SPEEDY SUMMER FRUIT SALAD

10 MINS OR LESS!

Dressing this fruit salad in a refreshing lemon and mint syrup helps the fruit stay fresh and colourful, and tastes delicious, too! This is lovely for a light breakfast – add a dollop of yogurt if you want something a little more filling.

SERVES 4-6 • **READY IN** 5 mins

- -

1 MAKE THE SYRUP

Put the sugar, lemon juice, and 2 tablespoons of water in a small, heavy-based saucepan, place over a low heat, and heat gently until the sugar melts. Cool, then stir in the mint.

2 MIX IT ALL UP

Mix all the fruit together in a bowl and toss it with the syrup. Chill until required, or eat straight away.

TIP – While you can use any combination of fruit, it's best to avoid bananas or really ripe raspberries, which will disintegrate when mixed with the other fruit.

INGREDIENTS

2 tbsp caster sugar

juice of ½ lemon

2 tbsp finely chopped mint leaves

½ small cantaloupe melon, peeled, deseeded, and cut into 1cm (½in) cubes

100g (3½oz) strawberries, halved or quartered, depending on size

50g (1¾oz) blueberries

50g (1¾oz) green, seedless grapes, halved

2 kiwi fruit, peeled and cut into 1cm (½in) cubes

WHEEL OF SMOOTHIES

What better way to start your day than with a delicious hit of vitamins and energy from a speedy smoothie? This wheel presents hundreds of exciting combinations – use it to inspire your next tasty blend.

MAKE YOUR SMOOTHIE

Use the ingredient suggestions as a guide, then adjust to taste. So if you want to use two liquids or no veg, for example, that's fine! The quantities are for 1 serving.

- -

1

CHOOSE YOUR LIQUID
Add it to the blender.

2

ADD A THICKENER
If you want a more substantial smoothie.

3

POP IN SOME VEG
Such as leafy greens or summer squashes.

4

ADD YOUR FRUITY INGREDIENT
Or make fruit the star of the show.

5

THROW IN THE EXTRAS
Add your choice of flavourings and garnishes.

6

WHIZZ IT ALL UP
Blend to your desired consistency. Serve in a glass or pour into a bottle to drink on the go.

Start small with the flavourings – then taste your smoothie and add more, if you like.

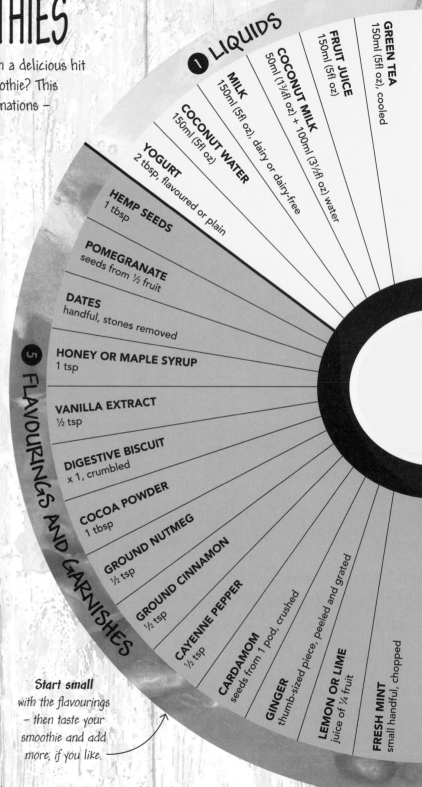

1 LIQUIDS

GREEN TEA
150ml (5fl oz), cooled

FRUIT JUICE
150ml (5fl oz)

COCONUT MILK
50ml (1¾fl oz) + 100ml (3½fl oz) water

MILK
150ml (5fl oz), dairy or dairy-free

COCONUT WATER
150ml (5fl oz)

YOGURT
2 tbsp, flavoured or plain

5 FLAVOURINGS AND GARNISHES

HEMP SEEDS
1 tbsp

POMEGRANATE
seeds from ½ fruit

DATES
handful, stones removed

HONEY OR MAPLE SYRUP
1 tsp

VANILLA EXTRACT
½ tsp

DIGESTIVE BISCUIT
x 1, crumbled

COCOA POWDER
1 tbsp

GROUND NUTMEG
½ tsp

GROUND CINNAMON
½ tsp

CAYENNE PEPPER
½ tsp

CARDAMOM
seeds from 1 pod, crushed

GINGER
thumb-sized piece, peeled and grated

LEMON OR LIME
juice of ¼ fruit

FRESH MINT
small handful, chopped

② THICKENERS

- **BANANA** x 1
- **AVOCADO** x 1
- **CHIA SEEDS** ½ tbsp
- **OATMEAL** 1 tbsp
- **NUT BUTTERS** 1 tbsp

Chia seeds soon become gelatinous once wet, so it's best to drink a chia-based smoothie straight away.

Remove tough stalks from your leafy greens before adding to the blender.

③ VEGETABLES

- **SPINACH** large handful
- **SPRING GREENS** large handful
- **KALE** large handful
- **CHARD** large handful
- **CUCUMBER** x ¼ – ½
- **BROCCOLI** ¼ head
- **PUMPKIN OR SQUASH** 80g (3oz), cooked

④ FRUIT

- **MANGO** x ½, peeled and stone removed
- **PINEAPPLE** 1 large slice
- **STRAWBERRIES** 75g (2½oz), hulled
- **RASPBERRIES** 75g (2½oz)
- **BLUEBERRIES** 75g (2½oz)
- **KIWI FRUIT** x 2, skin removed
- **PEACHES** x 2, stones removed
- **NECTARINES** x 2, stones removed

TOP COMBOS

Here are a few of our favourite smoothie ideas, to get you started...

DREAMY PEACH
Vanilla yogurt • banana • strawberries • peaches • ground cinnamon • mint leaves

GREEN POWER
Almond or coconut milk • avocado • spinach • hemp seeds • lime juice

PUMPKIN PIE
Whole milk • cooked pumpkin • vanilla extract • ground cinnamon • crumbled digestive biscuit

JADE
Apple juice • cucumber • lemon juice • honey • mint leaves

NUTTY BLUE
Vanilla yogurt • milk • smooth peanut butter • blueberries • peaches • vanilla extract

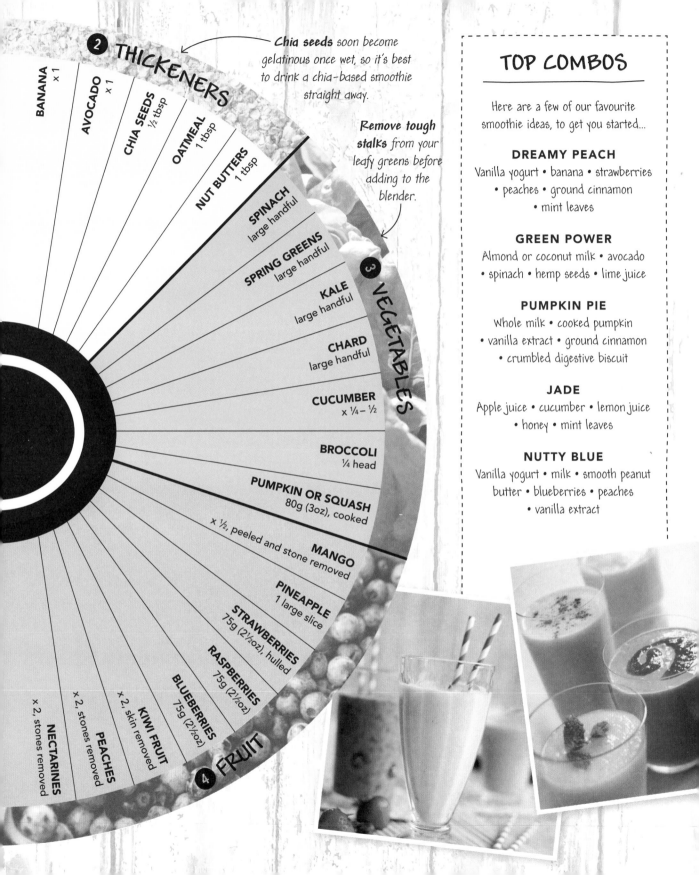

TROPICAL BREAKFAST SMOOTHIE

10 MINS OR LESS!

This quick and healthy smoothie uses frozen mango, which means the only preparation you have to do is peel and slice the bananas! For a creamier drink, use whole milk instead of apple juice.

SERVES 2 • **READY IN** 5 mins
SPECIAL EQUIPMENT Blender or hand-held blender

INGREDIENTS

- 1 banana, peeled and sliced
- 100g (3½oz) frozen mango cubes
- 4 tbsp Greek yogurt
- 1½ tbsp runny honey
- 250ml (9fl oz) apple juice
- ice cubes, to serve (optional)

1 WHIZZ THE INGREDIENTS
Place all the ingredients, except the ice cubes, in a blender and whizz until you have a thick, smooth drink, or blitz them with a hand-held blender.

2 SERVE WITH ICE (IF YOU LIKE)
Pour the smoothie into glasses to serve immediately. Add ice cubes if you like, or if it is a particularly hot day.

Try adding
2 tbsp rolled oats to the smoothie mix before blending for a filling "breakfast in a glass".

PLAN OF ACTION!

1 WHIZZ THE INGREDIENTS → **2 SERVE WITH ICE**

FROZEN FRUITY YOGURT LOLLIES

Who says ice lollies are just for kids? These fruity yogurt lollies, packed with vitamin-rich blueberries, are perfect for summery breakfasts on the go, or healthy hot-weather snacks.

MAKES 6–8 • **READY IN** 5 mins, plus freezing
SPECIAL EQUIPMENT Blender or hand-held blender • Lolly moulds

INGREDIENTS

- 500g pot of plain yogurt
- 200g (7oz) blueberries
- 75g (2½oz) icing sugar

1 WHIZZ THE INGREDIENTS
Place all the ingredients in a blender and whizz until smooth, or blitz them with a hand-held blender.

2 TRANSFER AND FREEZE
Carefully transfer the mixture to the lolly moulds and freeze for at least 2 hours (they will keep in the freezer for up to 8 weeks).

3 RELEASE AND SERVE
To serve, place the moulds under running hot water, carefully, for 1 minute to help release the lollies.

> **Try using other** soft fruits, such as strawberries, peaches, or raspberries in place of the blueberries for a range of flavours.

 PLAN OF ACTION!

1 WHIZZ THE INGREDIENTS → **2 TRANSFER AND FREEZE** → **3 RELEASE AND SERVE**

PERFECT PORRIDGE

For 1 serving, bring 50g (1¾oz) porridge oats, 150ml (5fl oz) whole milk, 200ml (7fl oz) water, and a pinch of salt to the boil. Reduce the heat and simmer, stirring constantly, for 7–10 minutes. For these variations, simply add the extra ingredients during cooking.

BLACKBERRY AND HONEY
Add 100g (3½oz) blackberries and 2 tbsp honey.

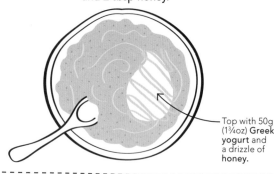

Top with 50g (1¾oz) **Greek yogurt** and a drizzle of **honey**.

MAPLE SYRUP, CINNAMON, AND APPLE
Add 3 tbsp maple syrup and 1 tsp cinnamon.

Top with slices of crisp **apple**.

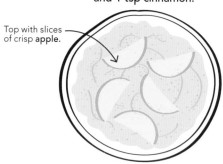

VANILLA AND PEACH
Add 2 tbsp brown sugar and 1 tsp vanilla extract.

Top with slices of **peach** and a sprinkling of **brown sugar**.

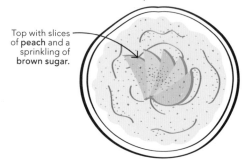

BLUEBERRY, FIG, AND ALMOND
Add 2 tbsp blueberry jam.

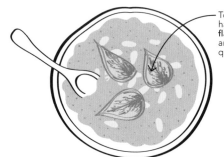

Top with a handful of **flaked almonds** and 1 fresh **fig**, quartered.

DAIRY-FREE PINEAPPLE AND PECAN
Use coconut milk instead of whole milk and add 100g (3½oz) pineapple chunks.

Toast a handful of **pecans** in 1 tbsp **coconut oil**, until golden brown, and sprinkle over, along with 1 tbsp brown sugar.

SPICED PUMPKIN
Add 50g (1¾oz) puréed pumpkin, 2 tbsp brown sugar, and 1 tsp each of cinnamon, grated nutmeg, ground ginger, and ground cloves.

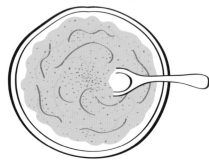

OVERNIGHT OATS

Leave these no-cook oats to soak in a sealed jar in the fridge overnight, then enjoy a delicious instant breakfast the next morning. Simply combine 50g (1¾oz) porridge oats, 350ml (12fl oz) liquid, and your choice of flavourings.

COCONUT AND BANANA
The rich, nutty coconut milk works perfectly with the comforting banana and chocolate.

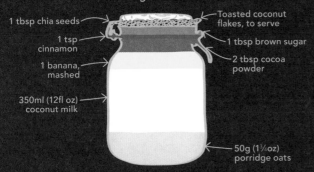

- 1 tbsp chia seeds
- 1 tsp cinnamon
- 1 banana, mashed
- 350ml (12fl oz) coconut milk
- Toasted coconut flakes, to serve
- 1 tbsp brown sugar
- 2 tbsp cocoa powder
- 50g (1¾oz) porridge oats

HONEY OATS WITH CHERRIES
The sweetness of the honey is balanced here by the tart cherries.

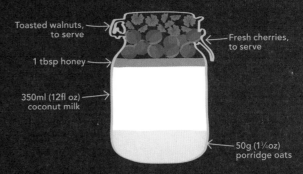

- Toasted walnuts, to serve
- 1 tbsp honey
- 350ml (12fl oz) coconut milk
- Fresh cherries, to serve
- 50g (1¾oz) porridge oats

CHOCOLATE AND HAZELNUT
A delicious combination for a sweet and decadent breakfast.

- 2 tbsp hazelnut spread
- 350ml (12fl oz) whole milk
- Toasted hazelnuts, to serve
- 50g (1¾oz) porridge oats

ALMOND AND PEACH
Almond milk, peaches, and oats make for an almost crumble-like dish.

- Squeeze of lemon juice, to serve
- 1 tbsp almond butter
- 350ml (12fl oz) almond milk
- Fresh peach slices, to serve
- 50g (1¾oz) porridge oats

STRAWBERRY DELIGHT
A simple yet delicious combination of fresh and preserved fruit.

- 1 tbsp strawberry jam
- 350ml (12fl oz) whole milk
- Fresh strawberries and blueberries, to serve
- 50g (1¾oz) porridge oats

CARROT CAKE OATS
If you're a fan of carrot cake, you'll love the flavours in these oats.

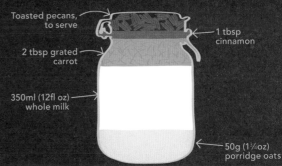

- Toasted pecans, to serve
- 2 tbsp grated carrot
- 350ml (12fl oz) whole milk
- 1 tbsp cinnamon
- 50g (1¾oz) porridge oats

INGREDIENTS

125g (4½oz) porridge oats

50g (1¾oz) mixed seeds, such as sunflower, sesame, pumpkin, and golden linseed

50g (1¾oz) mixed unsalted nuts, such as cashews, almonds, hazelnuts, and walnuts

1 tbsp light olive oil, plus extra for greasing

2 tbsp runny honey

3½ tbsp maple syrup

25g (scant 1oz) dried blueberries

25g (scant 1oz) dried cranberries

25g (scant 1oz) dried cherries

15g (½oz) desiccated coconut

Greek yogurt or milk, to serve

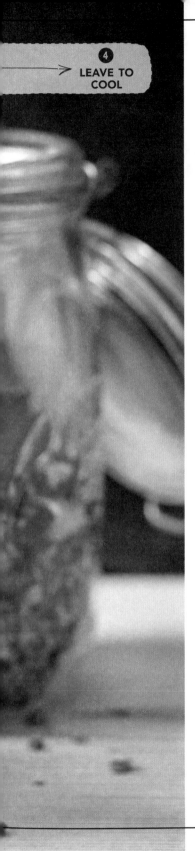

4
LEAVE TO
COOL

QUICK STOVETOP GRANOLA

Making your own granola ensures it's packed with your favourite ingredients, which you can mix and match to your heart's desire. For something a bit more decadent, try drizzling melted chocolate over the granola as it cools.

SERVES 4-6 • READY IN 15 mins, plus cooling

1 TOAST THE OATS, SEEDS, AND NUTS

Place the oats, seeds, and nuts in a large deep-sided frying pan. Heat over a medium heat, stirring frequently, for 3–5 minutes, or until lightly browned. Tip onto a baking tray and set aside.

2 ADD THE OIL, HONEY, AND SYRUP

Heat the oil, honey, and syrup in the frying pan until melted and well combined. Return the toasted oats, seeds, and nuts to the pan and heat for a further 5 minutes, stirring frequently, until warmed through and evenly coated.

3 COMBINE WITH THE DRIED FRUIT

Mix together the berries, cherries, and coconut, add to the pan, and combine well.

4 LEAVE TO COOL

Tip the mixture onto the baking tray, spread it out, and leave to cool completely. When cold, break the granola into small pieces and transfer to an airtight container. To serve, layer Greek yogurt and granola into 4 glass dishes. Alternatively, serve with milk.

TIP – This keeps for up to a month in an airtight container. As it gets older, it may benefit from a brief reheating in the oven to crisp up once more.

For lots more granola ideas, see pp32–33.

GRANOLA BLENDS

Do you like your granola sweet and fruity, savoury and nutty, or somewhere in between? To create your own perfect blend, use the ingredient and proportion suggestions below, then follow the cooking instructions on pages 30–31. To make muesli instead, simply combine the dry ingredients and enjoy straight away.

DRY INGREDIENTS

Grains, typically rolled oats, form the base of most granolas and muesli. Buckwheat, a grain-like seed, is a great gluten-free option. Nuts and seeds add a wholesome crunch and dried fruit adds sweetness and a softer texture to the blend.

1 GRAINS
Add 3–4 parts of a single grain or a selection of **mixed grains**, such as **rolled oats**, **spelt**, **quinoa**, and **barley**. Try also: rye, buckwheat, or wheatgerm.

2 NUTS
If you like nuts, add 1–2 parts of a single nut or a selection of **mixed nuts**, such as **almonds, pistachios**, **pecans**, **hazelnuts**, and **brazil nuts**. Chop any that are too large. Try also: cashews, macadamias, peanuts, or walnuts.

3 SEEDS
If you enjoy seeds, add 1–2 parts of a single seed or a selection of mixed seeds, such as **pumpkin seeds**, **sesame seeds**, **sunflower seeds**, and **chia seeds**. Try also: hemp seeds, pine nuts, poppy seeds, or flaxseed.

4 DRIED FRUIT
To add sweetness, include 1–2 parts of a single dried fruit or a selection of **mixed dried fruit**, such as **cranberries**, **banana chips**, **mango**, and **dates**. Try also: cherries, apricots, figs, raisins, or sultanas.

WET INGREDIENTS, SPICES, AND FLAVOURINGS

Adding a fat binds the dry ingredients. Spices and flavourings are a delicious optional extra, and a syrup, spread, or preserve helps create sweet, crunchy clusters during cooking.

5 FATS
Add ¼–½ part of **olive oil**, sunflower oil, coconut oil, or melted butter.

6 SPICES AND FLAVOURINGS
Why not add a small amount of your favourite spice or flavouring, such as **ground cinnamon** or **vanilla extract**? Try also: grated nutmeg, ground ginger, allspice, almond extract, grated lemon or orange zest, or coconut shavings.

7 SYRUPS, SPREADS, AND PRESERVES
Add ½–1 part of your favourite syrup, spread, or preserve, such as **maple syrup**, **raspberry jam**, or **peanut butter**. Try also: honey, agave nectar, rice syrup, hazelnut spread, fruit jams and preserves, lemon curd, or apple sauce.

1 Mixed grains

2 Mixed nuts

7 Crunchy peanut butter

3 Mixed seeds

7 Raspberry jam

4 Mixed dried fruit

7 Maple syrup

6 Vanilla extract

5 Olive oil

6 Ground cinnamon

Serving suggestions

Serve with milk (either cow's milk or dairy-free options such as almond, soya, or coconut) or yogurt. Top with chopped fresh fruit, fresh berries, or a dollop of fruit compôte.

BANANA AND OATBRAN MUFFINS

These muffins are a tasty and healthy choice for a late leisurely brunch. There's no need to wait until they cool completely as they're delicious eaten still warm.

MAKES 12 • **READY IN** 20 mins
SPECIAL EQUIPMENT 12 paper muffin cases and 12-hole muffin tin • electric hand-held whisk

- 160g (5¾oz) plain flour
- 100g (3½oz) oatmeal
- 1 tsp ground cinnamon
- 1 tsp baking powder
- 1 tsp bicarbonate of soda
- 50g (1¾oz) chopped walnuts
- 110g (3¾oz) butter, softened
- 100g (3½oz) demerara sugar
- 2 eggs, lightly beaten
- 3 ripe bananas, mashed
- 120ml (4fl oz) whole milk

MIX DRY INGREDIENTS

MUFFIN CASES

1 LINE

MUFFIN TIN

2 SIFT

cinnamon
baking powder
bicarbonate of soda

SIEVE

oatmeal

flour and walnuts

Preheat oven to 190°C (375°F/Gas 5). Line the muffin tin with muffin cases.

Sift the flour, oatmeal, cinnamon, baking powder and bicarbonate of soda to aerate them and get rid of lumps. Tip in any oatmeal bran left in the sieve, add the walnuts, and stir well.

MIX WET INGREDIENTS AND COMBINE WITH DRY

ELECTRIC WHISK

sugar

butter

3 CREAM

Cream the butter and sugar together until very light and fluffy.

milk

mashed banana

eggs

4 ADD

Add the beaten eggs and mix well. Then stir in the bananas and milk.

wet mixture

dry mixture

5 POUR

Pour the wet mixture into the dry and stir until just combined (do not over-mix or the muffins will be heavy).

BAKE!

6 DIVIDE

Divide the mixture between the muffin cases, then place the tin in the oven and bake for 15–20 minutes.

7 CHECK

The muffins are ready when a cocktail stick inserted into one of them comes out clean. Transfer to a wire rack to cool.

To freeze the muffins, wait for them to cool, then place on a baking sheet and freeze. After about 3 hours, transfer to a freezer bag and seal. Defrost at room temperature.

LEMON AND POPPY SEED MUFFINS

These light and lemony muffins are perfect for a weekend breakfast or brunch – you can eat them straight away and pop the leftovers in an airtight container to have as sweet snacks throughout the week.

MAKES 12 • **READY IN** 20 mins, plus cooling
SPECIAL EQUIPMENT 12 paper muffin cases and 12-hole muffin tin

INGREDIENTS

- 250g (9oz) self-raising flour
- 1 tsp baking powder
- ¼ tsp salt
- 125g (4½oz) caster sugar
- finely grated zest of 1 lemon
- 1 heaped tsp poppy seeds
- 100ml (3½fl oz) whole milk
- 100ml (3½fl oz) plain yogurt
- 3½ tbsp sunflower oil
- 1 large egg, lightly beaten
- 2 tbsp lemon juice

FOR THE GLAZE

- 2 tbsp lemon juice
- 150g (5½oz) icing sugar
- finely grated zest of 1 lemon

1 MIX THE DRY INGREDIENTS

Preheat the oven to 200°C (400°F/Gas 6) and line a 12-hole muffin tin with paper muffin cases. Sift the flour, baking powder, and salt into a large bowl. Use a balloon whisk to mix through the sugar, lemon zest, and poppy seeds.

2 MIX WET INGREDIENTS AND COMBINE WITH DRY

Measure the milk, yogurt, and oil into a jug, then add the egg and lemon juice and beat it all together thoroughly. Pour the liquid into the centre of the dry ingredients and mix with a wooden spoon. Stop mixing as soon as the ingredients are combined as over-mixing can make the muffins heavy.

3 DIVIDE AND BAKE

Divide the mixture equally between the muffin cases and bake in the middle of the preheated oven for 15 minutes until the muffins are lightly brown and well risen. Remove from the oven and allow them to cool in the tin for 5 minutes before transferring to a wire rack to cool completely.

4 DRIZZLE WITH THE GLAZE

For the glaze, mix the lemon juice and icing sugar to a thin icing, drizzle it over the muffins, and sprinkle them with lemon zest.

PLAN OF ACTION!

1 MIX DRY INGREDIENTS → 2 COMBINE WET AND DRY INGREDIENTS → 3 DIVIDE AND BAKE → 4 DRIZZLE WITH GLAZE

QUINOA AND POLENTA MUFFINS

High in fibre, these savoury muffins will make a perfect start to your day. Top with eggs, bacon, and avocado for a filling and hearty breakfast that's loads tastier than toast!

MAKES 8 • **READY IN** 30 mins
SPECIAL EQUIPMENT 8 paper muffin cases and 8-hole muffin tin

INGREDIENTS

- 1 tbsp light olive oil
- 4 large eggs
- 8 bacon rashers
- large knob of butter, to serve
- 2 avocados, pitted and cut into thin slices, to serve

FOR THE BATTER
- 130g (4½oz) polenta
- 60g (2oz) wholemeal flour
- 150g (5½oz) quinoa, cooked according to pack instructions
- 1 tbsp baking powder
- ½ tsp baking soda
- ¾ tsp sea salt
- 250ml (9fl oz) milk
- 3½ tbsp light olive oil
- 1 tbsp honey
- 3 large eggs

❶ MIX THE DRY INGREDIENTS

Preheat the oven to 200°C (400°F/ Gas 6). Grease and line an 8-hole muffin tin with the paper cases. For the batter, place the polenta, flour, quinoa, baking powder, baking soda, and salt in a large bowl and mix to combine.

❷ MIX WET INGREDIENTS AND COMBINE WITH DRY

In a separate bowl, whisk together the milk, oil, honey, and eggs until well combined. Then gently fold the liquid mixture into the dry ingredients and mix until just combined (over-mixing can make the muffins tough).

❸ DIVIDE AND BAKE

Divide the batter equally between the 8 muffin cases and transfer the tin to the oven. Bake for about 20 minutes, or until a cocktail stick inserted into the centre comes out clean.

❹ PREPARE THE EGGS, BACON, AND AVOCADO

Meanwhile, heat the oil in a frying pan over a medium heat and fry the eggs. Then add the bacon rashers and fry until crisp. Split the muffins, top with some butter, and serve with the fried eggs, bacon, and avocado.

PLAN OF ACTION! ❶ MIX DRY INGREDIENTS → ❷ COMBINE WET AND DRY INGREDIENTS → ❸ DIVIDE AND BAKE → ❹ PREP EGGS, BACON, AND AVOCADO

TOAST TOPPINGS

Smoky aïoli, fried egg, and crispy bacon bits on toasted crusty bread

Very ripe fresh **figs**

Soft cheese, such as **brie** or soft **goat's cheese**

Soft cheese, figs, and prosciutto on a toasted bagel

For the **aïoli**, whizz 3 tbsp mayo, 2 cloves of garlic (crushed), and ½ tsp chipotle or smoked paprika in a food processor.

Wilt the **spinach** in a frying pan over a medium heat before draining off excess liquid.

Soft goat's cheese, pear slices, and honey on white toast

Wilted spinach, scrambled eggs, and feta cheese on toasted rye

Toast doesn't have to be on the side – it can take centre-stage, too! With a little imagination and a handful of ingredients you can transform the humble slice into a stand-alone sensation. Experiment with different breads as well as toppings for the ultimate open sandwich. Here are a few ideas to tempt your toast-loving taste buds!

Cream cheese, smoked salmon, red onions, tomatoes, and capers on toasted pumpernickel

Peanut butter, banana, crushed walnuts, cinnamon, and honey on white toast

Plain yogurt, peach slices, and honey on white toast

Drizzle of **olive oil**

Sea salt and freshly ground **black pepper**

Mashed avocado and slices of hard-boiled egg on multiseed toast

TOAST TOPPINGS | **SPEEDY BREAKFAST AND BRUNCH** | **39**

INGREDIENTS

4 tbsp cream cheese

4 slices of challah bread or brioche, each 2.5cm (1in) thick

4–6 strawberries, hulled and thickly sliced

2 eggs

50g (1¾ oz) light soft brown sugar

4 tbsp or 60ml (2fl oz) milk

½ tsp vanilla extract

½ tsp ground cinnamon

2 tbsp butter

honey, to serve

PLAN OF ACTION!

1 ASSEMBLE SLICES → 2 DIP IN EGG → 3 PAN-FRY SANDWICHES

STRAWBERRY-STUFFED FRENCH TOAST

This is a decadent and delicious take on the brunch classic, French toast. Here, the bread is sandwiched together with softened cream cheese and juicy strawberries, to make a deluxe version that's even tastier than the original!

MAKES 2 • READY IN 20 mins

1 ASSEMBLE THE SLICES

Spread 1 tablespoon of the cream cheese over each slice of bread. Top 2 bread slices with 2–3 strawberries each, then cover with the remaining bread slices to make 2 sandwiches.

2 DIP IN THE EGG MIXTURE

In a bowl, whisk together the eggs, sugar, milk, vanilla extract, and cinnamon with a hand whisk. Dip the sandwiches in the egg mixture, submerging them completely.

3 PAN-FRY THE SANDWICHES

In a frying pan, melt 1 tablespoon of butter over a medium heat. Pan-fry the sandwiches for 3–4 minutes on each side, or until golden brown. Add the remaining butter to the pan, as needed. Serve hot, drizzled with honey.

BUTTERMILK PANCAKES

Making American-style pancakes with buttermilk rather than whole milk makes for a deliciously light and airy texture. These are perfect fare for a lazy morning.

MAKES 20 • **READY IN** 10–12 mins

- 25g (scant 1oz) butter, melted and cooled, plus extra for frying and to serve
- 150ml (5fl oz) buttermilk
- 100ml (3½fl oz) whole milk
- 2 large eggs, lightly beaten
- 1 tsp vanilla essence
- 1 tsp baking powder
- 25g (scant 1oz) caster sugar
- 225g (8oz) self-raising flour, sifted
- maple syrup, to serve

PREPARE THE WET INGREDIENTS

1 MELT

SMALL SAUCEPAN

butter

Melt the butter over a low heat.

2 MIX

Add cooled melted butter.

milk

buttermilk

vanilla essence

2 eggs

JUG

You can use all whole milk in this recipe, rather than whole milk and buttermilk, if you prefer.

Measure the buttermilk and whole milk into a jug, then add the other wet ingredients. Whisk everything together with a fork.

MAKE THE BATTER

3 COMBINE

baking powder

caster sugar

WOODEN SPOON

Flour

Combine the dry ingredients.

4 MIX TOGETHER

wet mixture

WHISK

Pour the wet mixture into a well in the centre of the flour mixture and whisk together.

COOK IN BATCHES

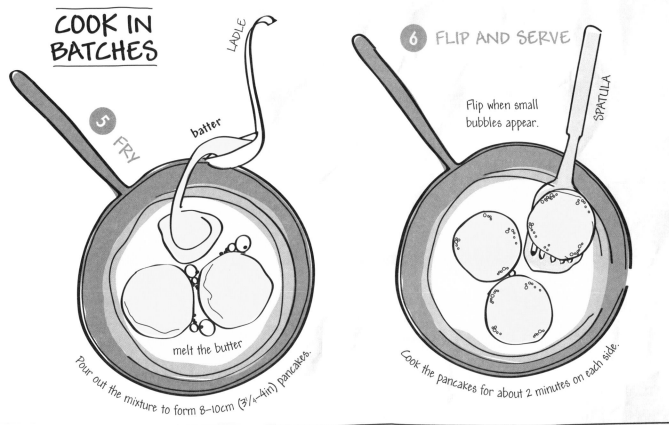

5 FRY

LADLE

batter

melt the butter

Pour out the mixture to form 8–10cm (3¾–4in) pancakes.

6 FLIP AND SERVE

SPATULA

Flip when small bubbles appear.

Cook the pancakes for about 2 minutes on each side.

PANCAKE TOPPINGS

For chocolate pancakes, add 3 tbsp **cocoa powder** and 4 tbsp **chocolate chips** to the batter.

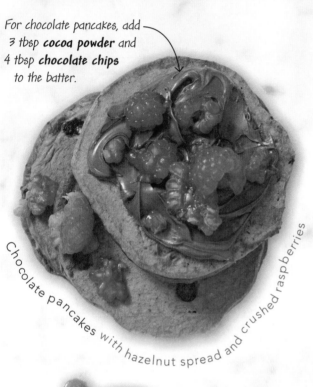

Chocolate pancakes with hazelnut spread and crushed raspberries

Mascarpone, peaches, and honey with fresh mint leaves

Very ripe fresh **peaches**

For the **caramelized banana**, melt 2 tbsp each of **butter** and **brown sugar**, add slices of **banana** and cook until golden brown.

Caramelized banana and crushed walnuts

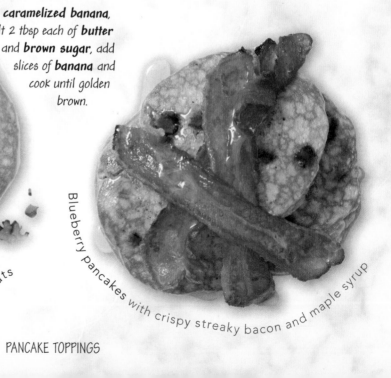

Blueberry pancakes with crispy streaky bacon and maple syrup

Blueberries and maple syrup are a firm favourite, but why not pile your pancakes with something a little different? Whether you want to satisfy your sweet tooth or have a soft spot for something savoury, here are some tasty and tempting topping ideas. See pages 42–3 for the basic pancake recipe.

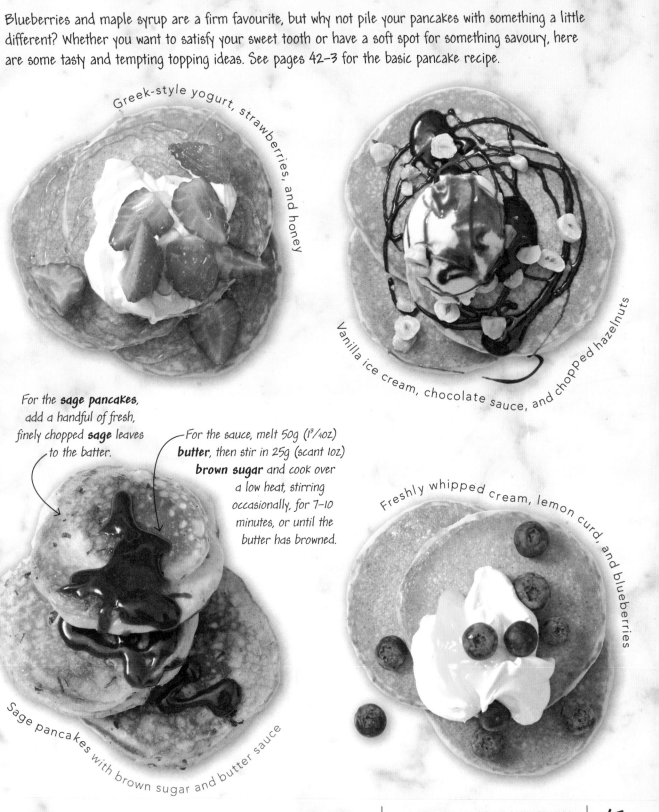

Greek-style yogurt, strawberries, and honey

Vanilla ice cream, chocolate sauce, and chopped hazelnuts

For the **sage pancakes**, add a handful of fresh, finely chopped **sage** leaves to the batter.

For the sauce, melt 50g (1³/₄oz) **butter**, then stir in 25g (scant 1oz) **brown sugar** and cook over a low heat, stirring occasionally, for 7–10 minutes, or until the butter has browned.

Freshly whipped cream, lemon curd, and blueberries

Sage pancakes with brown sugar and butter sauce

INGREDIENTS

225g (8oz) self-raising flour, sifted

1 tsp baking powder

25g (scant 1oz) caster sugar

150ml (5fl oz) buttermilk

100ml (3½fl oz) whole milk

2 large eggs

1 tsp vanilla extract

25g (scant 1oz) butter, melted and cooled, plus extra for frying, and to serve

150g (5½oz) blueberries

maple syrup, to serve

BLUEBERRY PANCAKES

This is the classic pancake combination. It's made here with tangy buttermilk for a lighter batter, but substitute whole milk if you prefer. If you've got friends over, why not take turns cooking and eating for a relaxed weekend brunch?

MAKES 20 • **READY IN** 20 mins

1 MIX THE DRY INGREDIENTS
Use a large balloon whisk to mix together the flour, baking powder, and sugar in a large bowl.

2 WHISK THE WET INGREDIENTS
Measure the buttermilk and milk into a jug, then add the eggs and vanilla extract and whisk it well. Whisk in the cooled, melted butter.

3 MAKE THE BATTER
Make a well in the centre of the flour and slowly whisk in the milk mixture, using the whisk to bring in the flour gradually from the edges of the well, until it has formed a thick batter.

4 ADD THE BLUEBERRIES
Heat a knob of butter in a frying pan and pour out 8–10cm (3¼–4in) pancakes. Once you have poured them into the pan, sprinkle some of the blueberries on top; the batter will rise up around the berries as they cook.

5 FRY AND FLIP
Fry the pancakes for 2 minutes on each side, turning when the edges are set and bubbles appear and pop on the surface. When cooked, keep them warm on a plate under a clean tea towel while you fry the rest. Serve with butter and maple syrup, or see pages 44–45 for more topping ideas.

TIP – Frozen blueberries are good value and work just as well as fresh fruit, so you can save money and cook these out of season, too. Add the berries straight from the freezer; they will defrost and cook at the same time as the pancakes and won't break down too much either.

Try adding
1 heaped tsp ground cinnamon to the batter for a spicy-sweet, aromatic flavour.

PUMPKIN AND CINNAMON WAFFLES

Adding spices and canned pumpkin to these waffles gives them a lovely autumnal flavour. If you can't find canned pumpkin purée, make your own by roasting and puréeing a fresh pumpkin.

SERVES 6 • READY IN 20 mins

SPECIAL EQUIPMENT Waffle maker or waffle iron

INGREDIENTS

- 200g (7oz) self-raising flour, sifted
- 50g (1¾oz) soft light brown sugar
- 1 tsp baking powder
- 2 tsp ground cinnamon
- 2 large eggs, separated
- 300ml (10fl oz) whole milk
- 1 tsp vanilla extract
- 50g (1¾oz) butter, melted and cooled
- 150g (5½oz) canned pumpkin purée
- maple syrup, sliced bananas, or fried apple wedges, to serve

1 MIX TOGETHER THE DRY AND WET INGREDIENTS

In a bowl, use a balloon whisk to mix the flour, brown sugar, baking powder, and cinnamon. Whisk in the egg yolks, milk, vanilla extract, melted butter, and pumpkin purée.

2 WHISK THE EGG WHITES

Preheat the waffle maker or iron. Using a clean whisk, whisk the egg whites to firm peaks. Stir the pumpkin mixture into the flour mixture until evenly combined.

3 BAKE THE WAFFLES

Preheat the oven to 130°C (250°F/ Gas ½). Pour a small ladleful of the batter onto the waffle maker or iron and spread almost to the edge. Close the lid and bake until golden. Keep warm in a single layer in the oven while you make the rest of the waffles.

4 SERVE IMMEDIATELY

Serve immediately with maple syrup, sliced bananas, or buttery fried apple wedges.

 **PLAN OF ACTION!** → **1 MIX DRY AND WET INGREDIENTS** → **2 WHISK EGG WHITES** → **3 BAKE WAFFLES** → **4 SERVE IMMEDIATELY**

CORNMEAL WAFFLES WITH BACON MAPLE SAUCE

These easy-to-make cornmeal waffles are a delicious twist on the brunch classic. The cornmeal adds a slight crunch and a delicate, moist sweetness to the waffles – a perfect base for the sweet-and-savoury sauce.

MAKES 6-8 • **READY IN** 20 mins
SPECIAL EQUIPMENT Waffle maker or waffle iron

INGREDIENTS

- 125g (4½oz) plain flour
- 50g (1¾oz) fine polenta or cornmeal
- 1 tsp baking powder
- 2 tbsp caster sugar
- 300ml (10fl oz) milk
- 75g (2½oz) unsalted butter, melted
- 1 tsp vanilla extract
- 2 large eggs, separated
- 4 smoked streaky bacon rashers
- 100ml (3½fl oz) good-quality maple syrup
- jam, fresh fruit, sweetened cream, or ice cream, to serve (optional)

1 MIX TOGETHER THE DRY AND WET INGREDIENTS

Place the flour, polenta, baking powder, and sugar in a bowl. Make a well in the centre and pour in the milk, butter, vanilla extract, and egg yolks. Using a balloon whisk, gradually whisk together the ingredients.

2 WHISK THE EGG WHITES

Preheat the waffle maker or iron. In a clean, large bowl, whisk the egg whites until soft peaks form. Fold into the batter with a metal spoon.

3 BAKE THE WAFFLES

Preheat the oven to 130°C (250°F/ Gas ½). Pour a small ladleful of the batter onto the waffle maker or iron and spread almost to the edge. Close the lid and bake until golden. Keep warm in a single layer in the oven while you make the rest of the waffles.

4 MAKE THE BACON MAPLE SAUCE AND SERVE

While the waffles are baking, make the sauce. In a frying pan, dry-fry the bacon until crispy. When cool enough to handle, crumble the bacon. Gently heat the maple syrup in a small, heavy-based saucepan over a low heat. Add the bacon to the warm syrup before pouring over the waffles. Serve immediately with jam, fresh fruit, sweetened cream, or ice cream, if desired.

PLAN OF ACTION! ➊ MIX DRY AND WET INGREDIENTS → ➋ WHISK EGG WHITES → ➌ BAKE WAFFLES → ➍ MAKE SAUCE AND SERVE

EGGS 6 WAYS

①	②	③
SOFT-BOILED	**POACHED**	**FRIED**

"SUNNY SIDE UP"

① Half-fill a pan with water and bring to a boil. Add a pinch of salt (this stops the white "leaking" if the shell cracks).

① Bring a large pan of water to a boil. Add a pinch of salt and a splash of white wine vinegar (to help bind the egg white).

① Melt a knob of butter or a splash of olive oil in a frying pan over a medium heat.

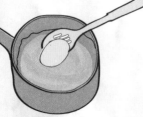

② Using a slotted spoon, carefully lower the egg into the water.

② Crack a very fresh egg into a small bowl.

② Crack an egg into the pan and fry for 5–6 minutes, or until the white has firmed. Season and serve hot.

"OVER EASY"

③ Boil for 4–6 minutes (depending on the size of the egg, and how runny you like the yolk).

③ Vigorously stir the water in the pan to create a vortex, then carefully pour the egg into the centre.

① For an egg fried on both sides, crack an egg into a heated greased pan (see step 1, above) and fry for 2–3 minutes.

④ Remove the egg from the pan and serve immediately.

④ Reduce the heat and cook for 2–4 minutes (depending on the size of the egg and how you like the yolk). Serve hot.

② Add salt to taste, then flip the egg, using a spatula, and fry for an additional 2 minutes. Serve hot.

Eggs are versatile, quick-cooking, and nutritious – ideal for a speedy breakfast or brunch. As well as trying these classic methods, why not add grated cheese, pieces of cooked ham, or sliced spring onion to your scrambled eggs – or pop some wilted spinach into the ramekins before cooking baked eggs?

④ EGG IN A HOLE	⑤ SCRAMBLED	⑥ BAKED

④ EGG IN A HOLE

❶ Use a 7.5cm (3in) round cookie cutter to cut a hole in the centre of a piece of toast.

❷ Melt a knob of butter in a frying pan over a medium heat and add the toast.

❸ Crack an egg into the hole and cook for 2–3 minutes. Add salt, to taste.

❹ Flip the toast and egg, using a spatula, and cook for an additional 2–3 minutes. Serve hot.

⑤ SCRAMBLED

❶ Crack 2–3 eggs into a large bowl. Add 2 tbsp water or milk, and salt and pepper to taste.

❷ Melt a knob of butter in a frying pan over a medium heat.

❸ Pour in the eggs and cook, stirring frequently with a wooden spoon, for 8–10 minutes, or until set.

❹ Serve hot, with toast.

⑥ BAKED

❶ Preheat the oven to 180°C (350°F/Gas 4) and bring 2 eggs to room temperature.

❷ Lightly grease 2 ramekins or egg coddlers. Crack an egg into each, and season with salt and pepper to taste.

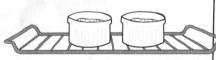

❸ Bake on the centre rack of the oven for 17–20 minutes, or until set.

❹ Remove from the oven and serve hot with buttered toast.

EGGS BENEDICT WITH BACON AND WALNUT BREAD

Crisp, salty bacon and crunchy walnut bread lift this breakfast classic to a whole new level. It's best enjoyed straight away, while the yolk and sauce are still hot and runny.

SERVES 2 • **READY IN** 15 mins
SPECIAL EQUIPMENT Blender or food processor

INGREDIENTS

FOR THE HOLLANDAISE SAUCE
- 100g (3½oz) unsalted butter
- 1 large egg yolk
- ½ tbsp lemon juice
- salt and freshly ground black pepper

FOR THE REST
- 6 smoked streaky bacon rashers
- 4 eggs
- 4 thick slices of walnut bread, or multigrain bread, crusts removed

1 MAKE THE HOLLANDAISE

Melt the butter over a gentle heat. Put the egg yolk, lemon juice, and seasoning into a blender and whizz briefly. With the motor running, pour in the melted butter drop by drop, accelerating to a thin stream, until the butter is fully combined with the other ingredients to create a thick sauce. Serve as soon as possible.

2 GRILL THE BACON

Meanwhile, preheat the grill on its highest setting. Cut each bacon rasher in half horizontally, to make 12 short rashers, and grill until crisp. Keep warm.

3 POACH THE EGGS

Boil a large pan of salted water, and reduce the heat to a low simmer. Crack an egg into a teacup and gently slide into the bubbling water. Repeat for all the eggs. Poach for 3 minutes, until the white is set but the yolk is still runny. Remove with a slotted spoon.

4 TOAST THE BREAD

Meanwhile, toast the bread. When toasted, top each piece with 3 half rashers of crispy bacon, a poached egg, and a little hollandaise sauce.

TIP – Use the freshest eggs you can find, as these will hold together better when you're poaching them. At step 3, use a spoon to stir the water so that a whirlpool forms, and tip the eggs into the centre. This helps keep the egg white together, as does adding a teaspoonful of vinegar to the boiling water.

If you fancy trying the original dish, eggs Benedict is traditionally made with ham and a toasted English muffin instead of bacon and walnut bread. Smoked salmon is also delicious in place of ham.

PLAN OF ACTION!
 MAKE HOLLANDAISE → **GRILL BACON** → ❸ **POACH EGGS** → ❹ **TOAST BREAD**

CROQUE-MADAME

This easy version of the French café staple uses three layers of melting Gruyère cheese in place of the traditional creamy sauce. It's the ultimate ham and cheese toastie!

MAKES 4 • **READY IN** 20 mins

INGREDIENTS

- 2 tbsp butter, plus extra for the bread
- 8 slices of good-quality white bread
- 200g (7oz) grated Gruyère cheese
- 1 tbsp Dijon mustard (optional)
- salt and freshly ground black pepper
- 4 thick slices of good-quality ham, or 150g (5½oz) thinly sliced ham
- 1 tbsp sunflower oil
- 4 small eggs

① ASSEMBLE THE SANDWICHES

Butter each slice of bread on both sides. Set aside 50g (1¾oz) of the grated cheese to top the sandwiches in step 3. Now make the sandwiches by spreading 4 slices of bread with a little mustard, if using, then a layer of grated cheese, firmly pressed down. Season with salt and pepper, then add a slice of ham, another layer of cheese, and a second slice of bread.

② BROWN THEM OFF

Melt the 2 tablespoons of butter in a large, non-stick frying pan and fry 2 sandwiches carefully over a medium heat for 2–3 minutes on each side, pressing them gently with a spatula, until golden brown. Keep warm while you fry the remaining 2 sandwiches. Wipe the pan with kitchen paper.

③ MELT THE CHEESE

Preheat the grill on its highest setting. Place the fried sandwiches on a baking sheet and top each with one quarter of the reserved grated cheese. Grill until the cheese has melted and is bubbling.

④ FRY THE EGGS

Meanwhile, heat the sunflower oil in the frying pan and fry the eggs to your liking. Top each sandwich with a fried egg and eat straight away.

PLAN OF ACTION! ① ASSEMBLE SANDWICHES → ② BROWN THEM OFF → ③ MELT CHEESE → ④ FRY EGGS

CROQUE-MADAME | SPEEDY BREAKFAST AND BRUNCH | 53

CLASSIC OMELETTE

The ultimate fast food, omelettes are extremely quick to make and very tasty, too – perfect for a nutritious and satisfying breakfast or brunch.

MAKES 1 • **READY IN** 5 mins

- 3 eggs
- salt and freshly ground black pepper
- knob of butter

BEAT AND SEASON EGGS

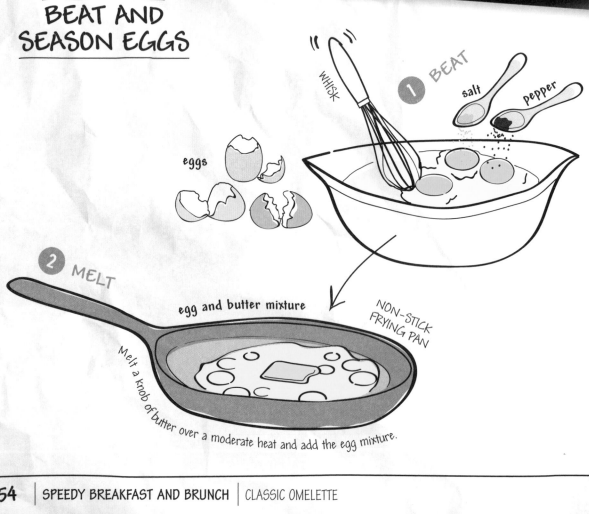

WHISK

1 BEAT

salt

pepper

eggs

2 MELT

egg and butter mixture

NON-STICK FRYING PAN

Melt a knob of butter over a moderate heat and add the egg mixture.

COOK EGGS

3 TILT

Tilt the pan to spread the egg mixture evenly. Stir the eggs with a fork, stopping as soon as they're set.

FORK

A 3-egg omelette is easiest to fold – any more than 6 will be more difficult.

FOLD AND SERVE

4 FOLD

half-folded omelette

Fold the side of the omelette nearest the handle halfway over itself.

5 TAP

neatly rolled omelette

Sharply tap the handle so the bottom side of the omelette curls over. Slide the omelette to the edge of the pan.

6 SERVE

PLATE

Tilt the pan over a plate so the omelette rolls "seam side" down.

CHEESE SOUFFLÉ OMELETTE

Why not jazz up an easy omelette by making it soufflé-style, with airy egg whites and oozy cheese? The lovely texture of the omelette is rapidly lost as it cools, so eat it straight away, with a green salad or crusty bread on the side, if you like.

MAKES 1 • READY IN 20 mins

1 MAKE THE SAUCE

Heat the butter in a saucepan. Add the corn and red pepper, stir, then cover and cook very gently for 5 minutes, or until tender. Stir in the cornflour, followed by the milk. Bring to the boil and cook for 2 minutes, stirring all the time, until thick. Stir in the chives, cheeses, cayenne, and salt and pepper.

2 PREPARE THE EGGS

Beat the egg yolks with 2 tablespoons of water and add salt and pepper. Whisk the egg whites until stiff and fold into the yolks with a metal spoon.

3 COOK THE OMELETTE

Preheat the grill. Heat a knob of butter in a non-stick frying pan, add the egg mixture, and gently spread it out. Cook over a medium heat for about 3 minutes until golden underneath. Immediately place the pan under the grill and cook for 2–3 minutes until risen and golden on top. Meanwhile, reheat the sauce, stirring.

4 FLIP, FOLD, AND GARNISH

Slide the omelette out onto a plate. Quickly spread one half with the cheese and corn sauce (don't worry if it oozes over the edge). Flip the uncovered side over the top to fold the omelette in half, and garnish with a few snipped chives. Serve immediately.

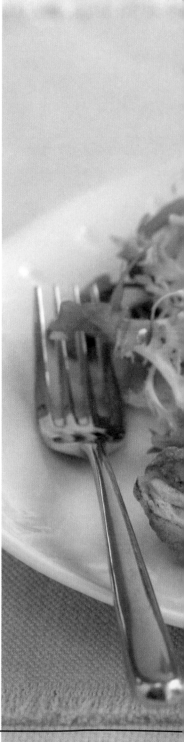

| ① MAKE SAUCE | → | ② PREPARE EGGS | → | ③ COOK OMELETTE | → | ④ FLIP AND FOLD |

INGREDIENTS

2 eggs, separated

knob of butter

FOR THE SAUCE
knob of butter

handful of fresh or thawed frozen sweetcorn kernels

½ small red pepper, deseeded and finely chopped

2 tsp cornflour

7 tbsp milk

2 tsp snipped chives, plus a few extra to garnish

20g (¾oz) Gruyère cheese, grated

20g (¾oz) Cheddar cheese, grated

pinch of cayenne pepper

salt and freshly ground black pepper

BREAKFAST BURRITOS

A great all-in-one breakfast, these American-style, Mexican-inspired burritos are perfect for a weekend brunch. If you've got leftovers, pop them in the fridge and microwave for an easy on-the-go weekday breakfast.

MAKES 4 • **READY IN** 20 mins

1 PREPARE THE FILLINGS

Preheat the grill on its highest setting and grill the bacon until it is crispy. Meanwhile, heat half the oil in a large, non-stick frying pan, add the potatoes, and fry until crispy all over, then set aside. Wipe the pan with kitchen paper. Mix the ketchup with the smoked paprika or harissa paste.

2 SCRAMBLE THE EGGS

Once the bacon and potatoes are ready, make the scrambled eggs. Whisk the eggs with the cream and season well. Heat the butter in the frying pan and cook the egg mixture over a low heat until they are barely cooked and still quite loose.

3 ASSEMBLE THE TORTILLAS

At the same time, lay out the tortillas and put 3 slices of bacon in a line across the middle of each. Top each with one-quarter of the potatoes, still keeping in a line across the centre, and add a smear of the spicy ketchup. Finish each by topping with one-quarter of the scrambled eggs and one-quarter of the cheese, again remembering to keep the filling in a compact rectangle down the middle of each tortilla.

4 ROLL THE BURRITOS

To make the burritos, tuck the sides in over the filling, then roll the longer top and bottom edges up and over the filling, to make a parcel. Press down gently.

5 BROWN THEM OFF

Heat the remaining 1 tbsp of oil in a clean frying pan. Put the burritos seam-side down into the pan and cook for 2–3 minutes over a medium heat, until golden brown and crispy. Press down with a spatula to seal the joins. Turn carefully and cook for 2–3 minutes. Depending on the size of your pan you may need to do this in 2 batches. Serve the burritos sliced in half on the diagonal, with extra spicy ketchup (if desired).

Fried sausage pieces, mushrooms, tomatoes, or even chillies are all great alternative fillings.

① **PREPARE FILLINGS** → ② **SCRAMBLE EGGS** → ③ **ASSEMBLE TORTILLAS** → ④ **ROLL BURRITOS** → ⑤ **BROWN THEM OFF**

INGREDIENTS

12 smoked streaky bacon rashers

2 tbsp sunflower oil

250g (9oz) cooked, cold potatoes, cut into 1cm (½in) cubes

4 eggs

6 tbsp tomato ketchup, plus extra to serve (optional)

1 tsp smoked paprika or harissa paste

1 tbsp double cream

salt and freshly ground black pepper

1 tbsp butter

4 x 20cm (8in) tortilla wraps

100g (3½oz) grated cheese, such as Cheddar

SHAKSHOUKA

This spicy, one-pot breakfast is popular across the Middle East. Serve it with crusty bread or flatbreads to mop up the egg yolks and the deliciously savoury sauce.

SERVES 4 • **READY IN** 20 mins

- 2 tbsp olive oil
- 1 onion, halved and finely chopped
- 2 red or green bell peppers, finely chopped
- 2 garlic cloves, finely chopped
- 1 red chilli, deseeded and finely chopped

- 1 tsp sugar
- 400g can chopped tomatoes
- salt and freshly ground black pepper
- 4 large eggs
- small bunch of flat-leaf parsley, finely chopped

FRY THE VEG

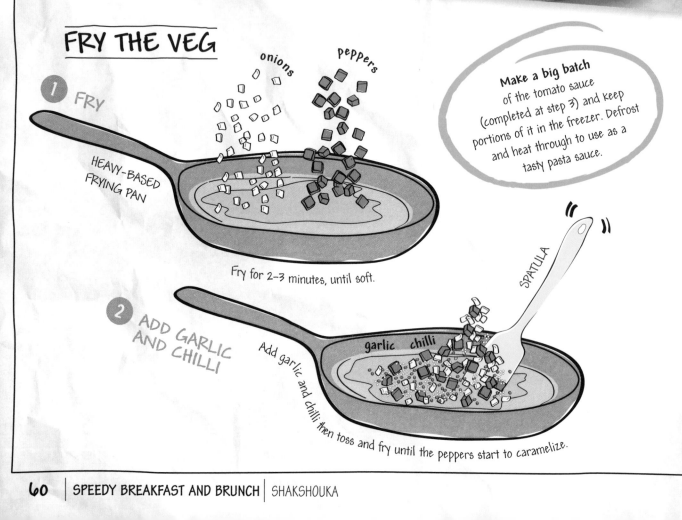

1 FRY

onions

peppers

HEAVY-BASED FRYING PAN

Fry for 2–3 minutes, until soft.

Make a big batch of the tomato sauce (completed at step 3) and keep portions of it in the freezer. Defrost and heat through to use as a tasty pasta sauce.

2 ADD GARLIC AND CHILLI

SPATULA

garlic   chilli

Add garlic and chilli then toss and fry until the peppers start to caramelize.

tomatoes

sugar

salt

pepper

COOK THE TOMATOES AND SUGAR OVER A MEDIUM HEAT FOR 3-4 MINS, THEN SEASON WELL WITH SALT AND PEPPER.

3 ADD TOMATOES

COOK THE EGGS

4 CRACK EGGS IN

eggs

Make indentations with a spoon.

Crack eggs into the indentations in the sauce.

5 COVER AND COOK

Cook until the egg whites are set and the yolks are done to your liking.

parsley

6 GARNISH AND SERVE

Remove the lid and scatter with chopped parsley.

POTATO, PANCETTA, AND RED ONION HASH

A hash is perfect if you fancy something a little more substantial in the morning. Try serving each portion topped with a fried egg – keep the yolks runny, if you like them that way, as they will form a "sauce" for the hash.

SERVES 2 • READY IN 20 mins

① **BOIL THE POTATOES**

Bring a pan of salted water to the boil, add the potatoes, and cook for 10 minutes. Drain.

② **FRY THE ONION, PEPPER, AND PANCETTA**

Meanwhile, heat the oil in a large, non-stick frying pan over a medium heat and cook the onion and red pepper for 5 minutes. Add the pancetta, season well, and cook for a further 5 minutes, stirring occasionally.

③ **BROWN THE POTATOES**

Add the boiled potatoes to the frying pan and cook over a high heat for about 10 minutes, stirring frequently.

④ **GARNISH AND SERVE**

Divide the hash between warmed plates, and sprinkle with the chives. Serve with a grating of Cheddar cheese or, if you prefer, baked beans and tomato ketchup.

TIP – This meal is a great way to use up leftover cooked potatoes – just cut them into bite-sized chunks and skip straight to step 2.

To add **warmth** to the dish, add 1 tsp of chilli powder or hot smoked paprika (pimentón picante) at step 2.

①	②	③	④
BOIL POTATOES	FRY VEG AND PANCETTA	BROWN POTATOES	GARNISH AND SERVE

INGREDIENTS

salt and freshly ground black pepper

500g (1lb 2oz) floury potatoes, such as King Edward or Maris Piper, peeled and cut into bite-sized chunks

2 tsp olive oil

1 red onion, finely chopped

½ red pepper, diced

50g (1¾oz) pancetta lardons

1 tbsp finely chopped chives

50g (1¾oz) grated mature Cheddar cheese, to serve

LUNCH IN A FLASH
OR ON THE GO

INGREDIENTS

4 large, crusty white
bread rolls

6 ripe, medium
tomatoes, sliced

½ small red pepper, cut
into thin strips

3 spring onions, white
parts only, sliced

4 hard-boiled eggs,
peeled and
sliced crossways

leaves from 1 small celery
head, chopped

16 small black olives,
pitted, kept whole
or halved

FOR THE VINAIGRETTE

6 anchovy fillets, packed in
oil or salt

12 tbsp olive oil

2½ tbsp red or white
wine vinegar

salt and freshly ground
black pepper

PLAN OF
ACTION!

1 MAKE
VINAIGRETTE ⟶ 2 ASSEMBLE
SANDWICHES ⟶ 3 FINISH OFF
AND SERVE

PAN BAGNA

This sandwich is sure to pep up your lunchbox repertoire! The vinaigrette dresses the fillings and moistens the bread, which explains its name – pan bagna means "bathed bread" in the local Provençal dialect.

SERVES 4 • READY IN 10 mins

- -

1 MAKE THE VINAIGRETTE

For the vinaigrette, drain and rinse the anchovy fillets, pat dry on kitchen paper, and chop finely. Place in a bowl and add the oil and vinegar. Stir well and season.

2 ASSEMBLE THE SANDWICHES

On a work surface, slice the bread rolls horizontally in half and place cut-sides up. Place a spoonful of vinaigrette on the bottom half of each roll and spread well. Add the tomatoes, red pepper, spring onions, eggs, celery leaves, and olives. Season lightly.

3 FINISH OFF AND SERVE

Spread the remaining vinaigrette over the top. Add the top half of each roll. Set on plates and press down each sandwich gently but firmly. Leave for 2–3 minutes, then cut in half and serve.

TIP – If you're making this for a lunchbox, pack the vinaigrette separately in a well-sealed container, and add to the sandwich just before eating. This will ensure that you don't have a soggy sandwich by the time lunch comes round!

SANDWICH SELECTOR

Mix fresh or canned **white crabmeat** with **lemon juice, black pepper,** sliced **apple,** and **micro greens.** For added kick, mix through some **harissa paste.**

Crab and apple on a toasted bagel

Roast beef on rye

For the horseradish mayo, mix 1½ tbsp **mayonnaise** with ½ tbsp **horseradish.**

Layer slices of cooked **roast beef, sweet red peppers, watercress,** and **horseradish mayo.**

For the honey chicken, brown ½ **chicken breast,** chopped, in a little **olive oil** over a medium heat. Stir in 1 tbsp **runny honey** and cook until caramelized.

Mix cooked, **shredded chicken** with **barbecue sauce,** and layer with sliced **avocado** and **rocket leaves.**

For the barbecue sauce, combine 2 tbsp **ketchup,** ½ tbsp each of **brown sugar, cider vinegar,** and **Worcestershire sauce,** and a pinch each of **sweet paprika, cayenne pepper,** and **garlic powder.**

Barbecue chicken on white

Combine the **honey chicken** with thinly sliced **red onion,** fresh **coriander,** and **sesame seeds.**

Honey chicken on a sesame seed roll

Transform the tired lunch-time staple into a truly gourmet experience with a little imagination and a few well-spent minutes. Light and fresh, rich and smoky, or crisp and crunchy – there's the perfect filling for every taste! Experiment with different breads, too.

Polish sausage on a baguette

Combine slices of **Polish sausage** with **sautéed onions** and **peppers**, and **wholegrain mustard**.

For the **onions** and **peppers**, sauté ½ **onion** and ½ **pepper** in a drizzle of **olive oil** with **salt** and **pepper** until soft.

Club sandwich on focaccia

Add layers of **smoky aïoli** (see p38), **Cheddar cheese with chilli**, cooked **turkey**, **roasted red peppers**, crispy **streaky bacon**, and fresh **spinach**.

Hummus and red pepper on multiseed

Layer **hummus**, sliced **cucumbers**, **red peppers**, and **alfalfa sprouts** (or **cress**, if you prefer).

Turkey and pesto on sourdough

Layer **pesto** (see p136), **havarti cheese** (substitute **Emmental** or **Edam**, if you prefer), cooked **turkey**, fresh **spinach**, and a dollop of **mayo**.

BEETROOT, GOAT'S CHEESE, AND ROCKET SANDWICHES

10 MINS OR LESS!

These are perfect for a picnic or packed lunch, or try them at home with toasted bread instead. Sweet, earthy beetroot is delicious with the more substantial texture of sourdough or rustic bread.

SERVES 4 • **READY IN** 10 mins

INGREDIENTS

- 8 large slices sourdough or other rustic bread
- butter, softened, for spreading
- 200g (7oz) soft goat's cheese
- freshly ground black pepper
- 4 small beetroot, pre-cooked and sliced
- 2 handfuls of rocket leaves

❶ PREPARE THE BREAD

Spread the slices of bread with butter on one side only. Spread 4 slices with one-quarter each of the goat's cheese, season with a little pepper, then add a layer of the beetroot slices.

❷ ASSEMBLE AND SERVE

Top the beetroot with a layer of the rocket and finish the sandwich with a final slice of bread, buttered-side down. Cut in half to serve, or pack into a container for transportation.

TIP – These sandwiches use pre-cooked beetroot to cut down on time (pickled or vacuum-packed both work well), but you can roast your own, if you prefer. Preheat the oven to 200°C (400°F/Gas 6). Cut 4 small beetroot (approximately 75g (2½in) each), into 5mm (¼in) slices. Place the slices on a baking tray, brush them with olive oil, and season well. Bake at the top of the oven for 20 minutes, turning once, until they are lightly browned and cooked through. Remove them from the oven and allow to cool before starting on step 1.

Why not try using roast or sundried tomatoes in place of the beetroot?

PLAN OF ACTION!

❶ PREP THE BREAD

❷ ASSEMBLE AND SERVE

BACON, LETTUCE, AND TOMATO SANDWICH

Zesty lemon and basil mayo lifts this BLT sandwich to another level. The classic sandwich combination remains a lunchtime favourite, and is perfect for the weekend – rather than a lunchbox – as the bacon is best served warm.

SERVES 1 • **READY IN** 15 mins

INGREDIENTS

- 3 slices of applewood or other good-quality bacon
- 2 tbsp unsalted butter, softened
- 2 thickly cut slices of good-quality bread
- 2 large cos lettuce leaves, roughly chopped and with stalks removed
- 1 medium tomato, sliced

FOR THE LEMON AND BASIL MAYO
- 2 tbsp good-quality mayonnaise
- 2 tsp lemon juice
- 1 tbsp finely chopped basil leaves
- salt and freshly ground black pepper

1 MAKE THE MAYO
Preheat the grill on its highest setting. To make the lemon and basil mayo, mix together the mayonnaise, lemon juice, and basil. Season with salt and pepper and set aside.

2 GRILL THE BACON
Preheat a griddle pan or a large, cast-iron frying pan. While it is heating, grill the bacon under the grill for 2–3 minutes on each side until crispy. Drain on kitchen paper and keep warm.

3 PREPARE AND TOAST THE BREAD
Spread a little butter on both sides of the bread slices and griddle them in the pan for 2 minutes on each side, until nicely toasted. Alternatively, omit the butter and simply toast the bread in a toaster.

4 ASSEMBLE AND SERVE
Remove the bread slices from the heat. Spread one side of the toast with a little of the mayonnaise, then top it with the lettuce, tomato, and the bacon. Finish with a final layer of mayonnaise and top with the second slice of bread. Cut in half to serve.

PLAN OF ACTION! ① MAKE MAYO → ② GRILL BACON → ③ PREP AND TOAST BREAD → ④ ASSEMBLE AND SERVE

INGREDIENTS

1 Cuban or French bread loaf

yellow mustard

4 slices of leftover roast pork

4 slices of ham

4 slices of Swiss cheese

4 pickled gherkins, sliced lengthways

butter, softened

PLAN OF ACTION!

① PREPARE SANDWICHES ⟶ ② TOAST AND SERVE

CUBANO

A Latin American variation of a toasted ham and cheese sandwich, pepped up with gherkins and mustard, the Cubano is one of the most popular street foods in Miami. Bring the streets to your kitchen with this make-at-home version!

SERVES 4 • **READY IN** 20 mins
SPECIAL EQUIPMENT Sandwich press or sandwich toaster

❶ PREPARE THE SANDWICHES

Cut the loaf into 4 x 15–20cm (6–8in) lengths, then slice each in half lengthways. Lightly coat 4 slices of the bread with mustard and layer each with 1 slice of the roast pork, ham, and cheese. Add a gherkin on top and cover with the remaining slices of bread. Brush the top of each sandwich with butter.

❷ TOAST AND SERVE

Place the sandwiches in a sandwich press or sandwich toaster, and press down until the cheese has melted and the outside of the bread is crisp. Remove from the grill, cut each sandwich diagonally across, and serve hot.

PRESSED CIABATTA WITH GRILLED VEGETABLES

This tasty loaf-sized sandwich is pressed and chilled to squash the fillings together and enhance the flavours. If you fancy it warm with the mozzarella melted, pop it in a sandwich toaster for a few minutes.

SERVES 4 • READY IN 20 mins, plus chilling

INGREDIENTS

- ½ aubergine, cut into 1cm (½in) slices
- 2 courgettes, cut into 1cm (½in) slices
- 4–6 tbsp olive oil
- salt and freshly ground black pepper
- 1 large beef tomato
- 1 ciabatta loaf
- 2 chargrilled red peppers from a jar, drained, and sliced
- ball of mozzarella, approx. 125g (4½oz), thinly sliced
- handful of basil leaves

❶ GRILL THE VEG

Preheat a large griddle pan or a grill on its highest setting. Brush the slices of aubergine and courgette on both sides with olive oil and season them well. Either griddle or grill them for 2–4 minutes each side, until they are charred in places and cooked through. Put them on a large plate in a single layer to cool.

❷ SLICE THE TOMATOES

Meanwhile, slice about 1cm (½in) off each end of the tomato, reserving these pieces. Slice the remaining tomato as thinly as possible.

❸ PREPARE THE CIABATTA

Cut the ciabatta in half, leaving a hinge so you can open it out flat. Drizzle both sides with a little olive oil. Take the offcuts of tomato and rub both sides of the bread with the cut sides of tomato, to soften and flavour the bread, then discard the tomato offcuts.

❹ ADD THE FILLINGS

Cover one side of the loaf with the red peppers and cooled slices of aubergine and courgette, then top with mozzarella. Sprinkle with the basil, season, then add the tomato.

❺ PRESS, CHILL, AND SERVE

Close the loaf and press down on it hard. Wrap it very tightly in cling film, going round it a few times until it is completely covered and compressed. Leave in the fridge with a weight (such as a chopping board and some full cans) on top for at least 4 hours, turning once. Unwrap and slice to serve, or transport in the wrapping and slice at a picnic.

PLAN OF ACTION!   ❶ GRILL VEG → ❷ SLICE TOMATOES → ❸ PREP CIABATTA → ❹ ADD FILLINGS → ❺ PRESS AND CHILL

STILTON RAREBIT WITH PEAR AND WALNUTS

A rarebit is a sophisticated version of cheese on toast, which uses a rich, savoury cheese sauce as a topping. Serve with this peppery-sweet, nutty salad for a delicious lunch or filling snack.

SERVES 4 • READY IN 20 mins

INGREDIENTS

- 4–8 slices walnut bread
- 1 shallot, finely chopped
- 75ml (2½fl oz) dry cider
- 30g (1oz) butter
- 30g (1oz) plain flour
- 150ml (5fl oz) milk
- 100g (3½oz) Stilton cheese, crumbled
- 50g (1¾oz) Cheddar cheese, grated
- 1 tsp English mustard
- 2 egg yolks
- 2 ripe pears, cored and sliced
- small bunch of watercress
- 60g (2oz) walnuts, broken into pieces
- 1 tbsp balsamic vinegar
- 2 tbsp extra virgin olive oil
- freshly ground black pepper

❶ TOAST THE BREAD
Lightly toast the bread; allow 1 or 2 slices per person, depending on the size of the slices.

❷ REDUCE THE CIDER
Meanwhile, place the shallot and cider in a small saucepan and simmer over a low heat until the cider has almost completely evaporated. Remove from the pan and set aside.

❸ MAKE THE CHEESE SAUCE
Wash the pan and add the butter. Place over a medium-low heat until melted, then stir in the flour. Cook, stirring, for 1 minute, then remove the pan from the heat and gradually stir in the milk. Return to the heat and cook for 2–3 minutes, or until thickened, stirring constantly. Add the cheeses and stir until melted. Remove from the heat and stir in the mustard, egg yolks, and cooled shallot. Spread the mixture thickly on to each toasted bread slice.

❹ GRILL THE TOASTS
Preheat the grill on its highest setting, then grill the toasts for 2 minutes, or until golden and bubbling.

❺ GARNISH AND SERVE
Arrange the pears, watercress, and walnuts on 4 plates, drizzle with a little balsamic vinegar and olive oil, and season with pepper. Place the toasts alongside and serve at once.

PLAN OF ACTION!

 TOAST BREAD → REDUCE CIDER → MAKE CHEESE SAUCE → GRILL TOASTS → ❺ GARNISH AND SERVE

FUSS-FREE FALAFEL

Using a can of chickpeas, instead of dried chickpeas soaked in advance, will give you all the flavour with none of the fuss in this Middle Eastern classic.

MAKES 12 • **READY IN** 20 mins, plus standing
SPECIAL EQUIPMENT Food processor

- 400g can of chickpeas
- 1 tbsp tahini
- 1 garlic clove, crushed
- 1 tsp salt
- 1 tsp ground cumin
- 1 tsp turmeric
- 1 tsp ground coriander
- ½ tsp cayenne pepper
- 2 tbsp finely chopped flat-leaf parsley

- juice of 1 small lemon
- vegetable oil, for frying

TO SERVE
- 4 pitta breads, warmed
- 1 Romaine lettuce, shredded
- 200g pot Greek yogurt
- ½ small cucumber, diced

PREPARE INGREDIENTS

1 DRAIN

TAP

chickpeas

COLANDER

Drain the chickpeas and rinse them under cold running water.

2 ADD

crushed garlic

tahini

salt

cumin

turmeric

ground coriander

cayenne pepper

Place ingredients in food processor bowl.

MAKE AND SHAPE

3 WHIZZ

FOOD PROCESSOR

Whizz the mixture in a food processor until finely chopped but not puréed.

TRANSFER TO A BOWL, COVER, AND SET ASIDE IN THE FRIDGE FOR AT LEAST 30 MINUTES.

4 SHAPE

Wet your hands and shape the mixture into 12 balls.

5 FLATTEN

Press down slightly to flatten.

FRY THE FALAFEL

6 FRY

WOK

Fry for 3–4 minutes, or until lightly golden.

Heat 5cm (2in) of oil and fry the falafel balls in batches.

SLOTTED SPOON

7 DRAIN

KITCHEN TOWEL

PITTA POCKETS

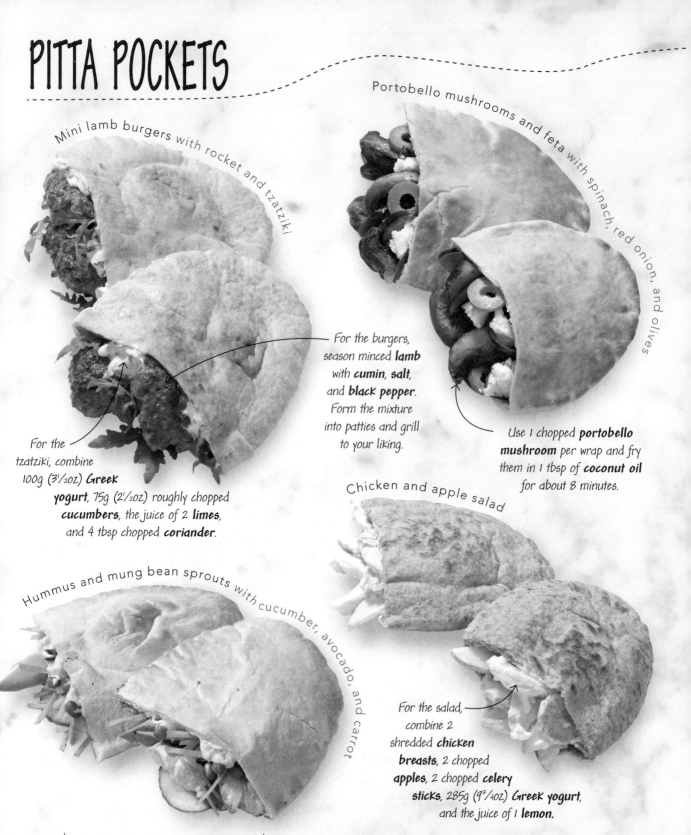

Mini lamb burgers with rocket and tzatziki

Portobello mushrooms and feta with spinach, red onion, and olives

For the burgers, season minced **lamb** with **cumin, salt,** and **black pepper.** Form the mixture into patties and grill to your liking.

For the tzatziki, combine 100g (3½oz) **Greek yogurt**, 75g (2½oz) roughly chopped **cucumbers**, the juice of 2 **limes**, and 4 tbsp chopped **coriander**.

Use 1 chopped **portobello mushroom** per wrap and fry them in 1 tbsp of **coconut oil** for about 8 minutes.

Chicken and apple salad

Hummus and mung bean sprouts with cucumber, avocado, and carrot

For the salad, combine 2 shredded **chicken breasts**, 2 chopped **apples**, 2 chopped **celery sticks**, 285g (9¾oz) **Greek yogurt**, and the juice of 1 **lemon**.

- - - - These pitta pockets – stuffed with a wide variety of healthy, tasty fillings – are a fast and fun alternative to more run-of-the-mill sandwiches. If you prefer your pitta breads warm, simply pop them in the toaster for 30 seconds to 1 minute, until puffed up but not crisp.

Shredded chicken in yellow curry sauce with red onion, avocado, and coriander

Tuna mayonnaise filling with micro greens and tomatoes

For the curry sauce, mix 200g (7fl oz) **Greek yogurt**, 50ml (1³/₄fl oz) **coconut milk**, 2 tbsp **yellow curry paste**, and 1 tsp **fish sauce**.

For the filling, combine 200g canned **tuna**, 50g (1³/₄oz) **mayo**, the juice of 1 **lemon**, 50g (1³/₄oz) chopped **gherkins**, and 75g (2¹/₂oz) chopped **red peppers**.

Honey and soy steak with onion and mangetout

Prawn and avocado with watercress

Pan-fry **steak** strips, sliced **onion**, and **mangetout** in **sesame oil** and coat with 3 tbsp each of **honey** and **soy sauce**, and 1 tbsp **sesame seeds**.

GAZPACHO

This chilled, no-cook Spanish soup is lovely for a hot day, or when you need a taste of summer! The vegetables are the stars of the show, so use the freshest you can find – the no-cook approach will celebrate their ripe flavour.

SERVES 4 • **READY IN** 15 mins, plus chilling
SPECIAL EQUIPMENT Food processor or blender

- -

1 PEEL AND CHOP THE TOMATOES

Bring a kettle of water to the boil. Place the tomatoes in a heatproof bowl, pour over enough boiling water to cover, and leave for 20 seconds, or until the skins split. Drain and cool under cold running water. Gently peel off the skins, cut the tomatoes in half, deseed, and chop the flesh.

2 WHIZZ UP INGREDIENTS

Place the tomato flesh, cucumber, red pepper, garlic, and vinegar in a food processor or blender. Season to taste and process until smooth. Pour in the oil and process again. Dilute with a little cold water, or a few ice cubes if too thick. Transfer the soup to a serving bowl, cover with cling film, and chill.

3 PREPARE THE GARNISHES

When ready to serve, finely chop the extra cucumber and red pepper. Place the cucumber, pepper, and egg yolk and white in individual bowls and arrange on the table, along with a bottle of olive oil. Ladle the soup into bowls and serve, letting each diner add their own garnish. If the soup hasn't had enough time to chill properly, add an ice cube or two to each bowl.

> **To make a more substantial meal**, add cubes of stale bread, soaked in olive oil and a dash of sherry vinegar, at step 2.
> **For a seafood twist**, try adding 115g (4oz) small cooked, peeled prawns (thawed if frozen) into the serving bowls at step 3.

INGREDIENTS

1kg (2¼lb) tomatoes, plus extra to serve

1 small cucumber, peeled and finely chopped, plus extra to serve

1 small red pepper, deseeded and chopped, plus extra to serve

2 garlic cloves, crushed

4 tbsp sherry vinegar

salt and freshly ground black pepper

120ml (4fl oz) extra virgin olive oil, plus extra to serve

1 hard-boiled egg, white and yolk separated and chopped, to serve

SWEET POTATO SOUP

This sophisticated soup is rich and velvety, and can be ready in minutes. The crispy croutons add a satisfying crunch and make this hearty dish even more substantial.

SERVES 4-6 • **READY IN** 20 mins
SPECIAL EQUIPMENT hand-held blender

- 5 tbsp olive oil
- 1 onion, chopped
- 1 leek, white part only, chopped
- 1 celery stick, chopped
- 500g (1lb 2oz) sweet potatoes, peeled and cut into 2.5cm (1in) cubes
- 750ml (1¼ pints) vegetable or chicken stock
- ½ tbsp chopped sage leaves
- salt and freshly ground black pepper
- 4 slices of day-old white bread, crusts removed and cut into 1cm (½in) dice
- 30g (1oz) unsalted butter

PREPARE THE SOUP

1 SOFTEN

onion

leek

celery

olive oil

Heat 3 tbsp of the oil and cook the veg for 5 minutes until softened but not browned.

2 ADD

salt

pepper

sweet potato

sage

liquid stock

Bring to the boil.

WHILE THE SOUP IS SIMMERING, PREPARE THE CROUTONS.

3 SIMMMER

SAUCEPAN LID

Reduce the heat to a gentle simmer, cover, and cook for 10 minutes, or until the sweet potato is tender.

MAKE THE CROUTONS

bread dice

WOODEN SPOON

LARGE FRYING PAN

4 FRY

olive oil and unsalted butter

Heat the oil and butter until hot, add the
bread dice, then fry, stirring constantly.

SLOTTED SPOON

KITCHEN PAPER

5 DRAIN

Fry the croutons for 10 minutes, or until golden, then
remove with a slotted spoon and drain on kitchen paper.

BLEND AND SERVE

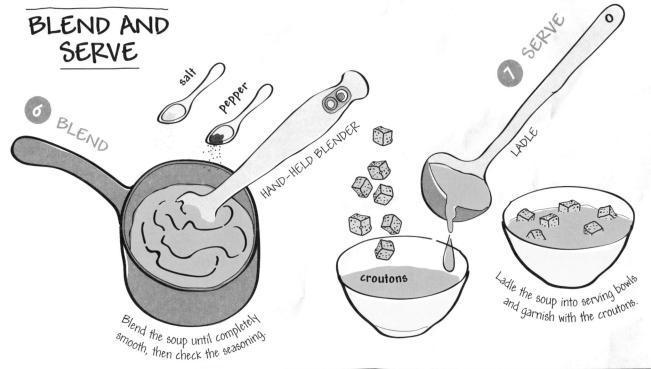

salt

pepper

HAND-HELD BLENDER

6 BLEND

Blend the soup until completely
smooth, then check the seasoning.

7 SERVE

LADLE

croutons

Ladle the soup into serving bowls
and garnish with the croutons.

SOPA AL CUARTO DE HORA

The Spanish name of this dish translates as "15-minute soup" because that's how long it takes to cook! It's ideal for when you want a nourishing meal in no time. Why not serve this flavoursome broth with toasted bread for dunking.

SERVES 4 • READY IN 20 mins

- -

1 SIMMER THE RICE

In a large pan, bring the broth, rice, and ham to the boil. Reduce the heat and simmer for 15 minutes, or until the rice is nearly tender.

2 ADD THE EGGS AND HERBS

Add the eggs and simmer for a further 1 minute. Remove from the heat, then stir in the parsley and mint, if using. Serve piping hot.

TIP – You can cut down the preparation time by using pre-cooked leftover rice, or by replacing the rice with soup pasta, such as vermicelli or ditalini.

PLAN OF ACTION!

① **SIMMER RICE** → ② **ADD EGGS**

INGREDIENTS

1 litre (1¾ pints) hot chicken or beef broth, fresh or from powdered stock

2 tbsp rice

4 tbsp diced Serrano ham

2 eggs, hard-boiled and chopped

1 tbsp finely chopped flat-leaf parsley

1 tbsp finely chopped mint (optional)

SUMMER PEA, MINT, AND QUINOA SOUP

This light and creamy chilled soup is enhanced by the addition of protein-packed quinoa and nutty-flavoured almond milk. Quick and easy to prepare, it makes the perfect summer lunch.

SERVES 4 • **READY IN** 20–25 mins, plus cooling
SPECIAL EQUIPMENT Food processor

INGREDIENTS

- 50g (1¾oz) uncooked quinoa
- 2 avocados, pitted
- 500g (1lb 2oz) frozen peas
- 20g (¾oz) chopped mint, plus extra to garnish
- 1 litre (1¾ pints) unsweetened almond milk

① PREPARE THE QUINOA

Rinse the quinoa under running water, drain, and place in a lidded saucepan. Cover with 250ml (9fl oz) of water and bring to the boil.

② COOK THE QUINOA

Reduce the heat to a simmer, cover, and cook for 15–20 minutes, or until almost all the liquid has been absorbed and the quinoa is fluffy. Remove from the heat, drain any remaining water, and set aside to cool.

③ BLEND THE AVOCADOS, PEAS, MINT, AND MILK

While the quinoa is cooking, scoop out the flesh from the avocados and place in a food processor. Add the peas, mint, and half the milk and whizz until smooth. Then add the remaining milk and whizz until fully blended.

④ DIVIDE AND SERVE

Divide the soup equally between 4 soup bowls. Top with equal quantities of the cooled quinoa. Garnish with some mint and serve immediately.

> **You can substitute** cow's milk for the almond milk, if you like.

PLAN OF ACTION! ① **PREPARE QUINOA** → ② **COOK QUINOA** → ③ **BLEND INGREDIENTS** → ④ **DIVIDE AND SERVE**

PARMESAN BROTH

This elegant pick-me-up enjoyed in Rome – where it is known as "stracciatella alla romana" – is made by swirling raw egg beaten with grated Parmesan cheese into boiling chicken broth.

SERVES 4-5 • **READY IN** 20 mins

INGREDIENTS

- 2 litres (3½ pints) hot chicken stock
- salt
- 4–5 eggs
- 2 tbsp finely grated Parmesan cheese
- 1 tsp freshly grated nutmeg
- grated zest of 1 lemon
- 2 tbsp finely chopped flat-leaf parsley

1 REDUCE THE STOCK

In a large saucepan, bring the chicken stock to the boil and allow it to bubble up until reduced by one-third. Season with salt.

2 WHISK THE EGGS AND CHEESE TOGETHER

In a bowl, whisk the eggs with the Parmesan, nutmeg, and lemon zest, until well-blended.

3 COMBINE THE STOCK AND EGG MIXTURE

Reduce the heat to a steady simmer and whisk in the egg mixture. Continue to whisk for a further 1–2 minutes as the egg forms fine pasta-like threads.

4 TASTE, GARNISH, AND SERVE

Taste the broth and add more cheese and seasoning, if you like. Garnish with parsley.

> **You could also** add diced prosciutto, finely chopped parsley, and a few scraps of deseeded peperoncino pepper to the soup, if you like.

 **PLAN OF ACTION!** **1 REDUCE STOCK** →  **2 WHISK EGGS AND CHEESE** →  **3 COMBINE STOCK AND EGG MIXTURE** →  **4 TASTE, GARNISH, AND SERVE**

SALAD-IN-A-JAR

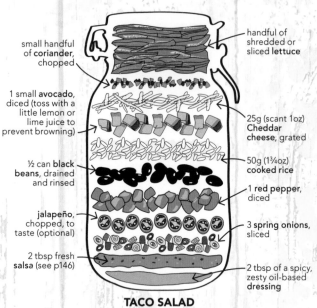

small handful of **coriander**, chopped

1 small **avocado**, diced (toss with a little lemon or lime juice to prevent browning)

½ can **black beans**, drained and rinsed

jalapeño, chopped, to taste (optional)

2 tbsp fresh **salsa** (see p146)

handful of shredded or sliced **lettuce**

25g (scant 1oz) **Cheddar cheese**, grated

50g (1¾oz) **cooked rice**

1 **red pepper**, diced

3 **spring onions**, sliced

2 tbsp of a spicy, zesty oil-based **dressing**

TACO SALAD
A taste of Tex-Mex in a jar, this salad is perfect for when you want a chilli hit.

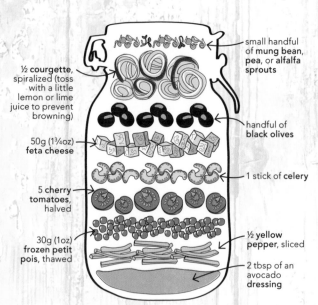

½ **courgette**, spiralized (toss with a little lemon or lime juice to prevent browning)

50g (1¾oz) **feta cheese**

5 **cherry tomatoes**, halved

30g (1oz) **frozen petit pois**, thawed

small handful of **mung bean, pea, or alfalfa sprouts**

handful of **black olives**

1 stick of **celery**

½ **yellow pepper**, sliced

2 tbsp of an avocado **dressing**

COURGETTI AVOCADO SALAD
Use a spiralizer or julienne peeler to make courgette spaghetti.

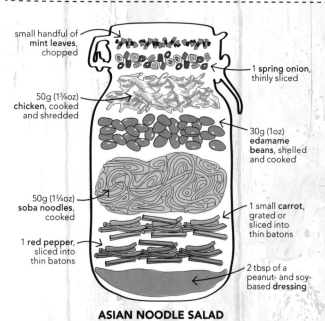

small handful of **mint leaves**, chopped

50g (1¾oz) **chicken**, cooked and shredded

50g (1¾oz) **soba noodles**, cooked

1 **red pepper**, sliced into thin batons

1 **spring onion**, thinly sliced

30g (1oz) **edamame beans**, shelled and cooked

1 small **carrot**, grated or sliced into thin batons

2 tbsp of a peanut- and soy-based **dressing**

ASIAN NOODLE SALAD
A zingy salad that combines flavours from Japan and Thailand.

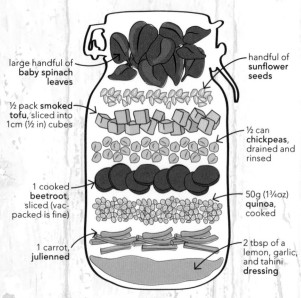

large handful of **baby spinach leaves**

½ pack **smoked tofu**, sliced into 1cm (½ in) cubes

1 cooked **beetroot**, sliced (vac-packed is fine)

1 **carrot**, julienned

handful of **sunflower seeds**

½ can **chickpeas**, drained and rinsed

50g (1¾oz) **quinoa**, cooked

2 tbsp of a lemon, garlic, and tahini **dressing**

QUINOA TOFU SALAD
Prepare this nourishing salad for a tasty, plant-based protein boost.

A speedy salad-in-a-jar makes an easy, transportable lunch. Layering the ingredients in the right order will prevent the dressing spreading and turning the greens soggy. When you're ready to eat, simply tip the jar upside down and shake to combine. See pages 90–91 for dressing ideas.

handful of **baby spinach leaves**

small handful of **basil**, torn

a few **sun-dried tomatoes**, chopped

8 **cherry tomatoes**, halved

50g (1¾oz) **mozzarella**, chopped into bite-sized pieces

75g (2½oz) cooked **pasta**, such as penne

2 tbsp **pesto** (see p136)

CAPRESE PASTA SALAD

A simple, fragrant salad that's great for using up leftover pasta.

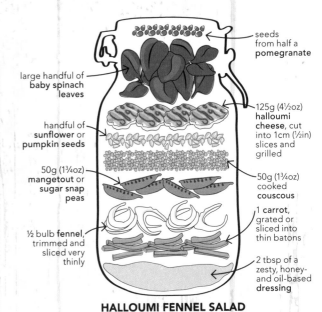

seeds from half a **pomegranate**

large handful of **baby spinach leaves**

125g (4½oz) **halloumi cheese**, cut into 1cm (½in) slices and grilled

handful of **sunflower** or **pumpkin seeds**

50g (1¾oz) cooked **couscous**

50g (1¾oz) **mangetout** or **sugar snap peas**

1 **carrot**, grated or sliced into thin batons

½ bulb **fennel**, trimmed and sliced very thinly

2 tbsp of a zesty, honey- and oil-based **dressing**

HALLOUMI FENNEL SALAD

Pair rich, salty halloumi with crisp raw veg for a satisfying lunch.

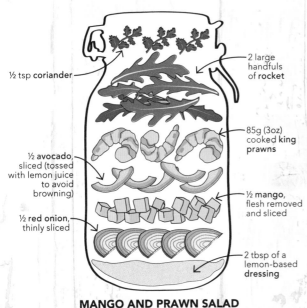

½ tsp **coriander**

2 large handfuls of **rocket**

a few **sun-dried** –

½ **avocado**, sliced (tossed with lemon juice to avoid browning)

85g (3oz) cooked **king prawns**

½ **mango**, flesh removed and sliced

½ **red onion**, thinly sliced

2 tbsp of a lemon-based **dressing**

MANGO AND PRAWN SALAD

A refreshing salad for a hot day – add a squeeze of lime, if you like.

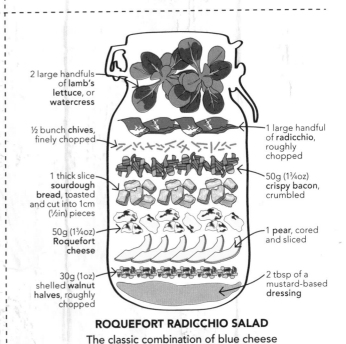

2 large handfuls of **lamb's lettuce**, or **watercress**

1 large handful of **radicchio**, roughly chopped

½ bunch **chives**, finely chopped

50g (1¾oz) **crispy bacon**, crumbled

1 thick slice **sourdough bread**, toasted and cut into 1cm (½in) pieces

50g (1¾oz) **Roquefort cheese**

1 **pear**, cored and sliced

30g (1oz) shelled **walnut** halves, roughly chopped

2 tbsp of a mustard-based **dressing**

ROQUEFORT RADICCHIO SALAD

The classic combination of blue cheese with apples and walnuts.

WHEEL OF SALAD DRESSINGS

Use this wheel to experiment with your own dressing ideas and give any salad a speedy makeover. To test your combo, dip a piece of lettuce in, shaking off the excess. This will give you a better idea of how it tastes than by dipping in a finger – and if it's not quite right you won't ruin the whole salad!

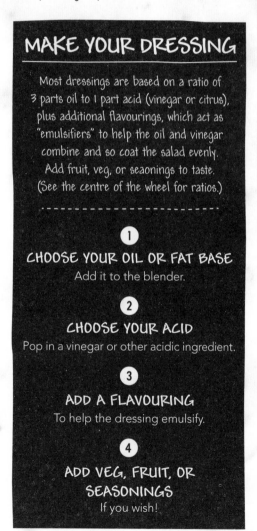

MAKE YOUR DRESSING

Most dressings are based on a ratio of 3 parts oil to 1 part acid (vinegar or citrus), plus additional flavourings, which act as "emulsifiers" to help the oil and vinegar combine and so coat the salad evenly. Add fruit, veg, or seaonings to taste. (See the centre of the wheel for ratios.)

- -

①

CHOOSE YOUR OIL OR FAT BASE
Add it to the blender.

②

CHOOSE YOUR ACID
Pop in a vinegar or other acidic ingredient.

③

ADD A FLAVOURING
To help the dressing emulsify.

④

ADD VEG, FRUIT, OR SEASONINGS
If you wish!

Why not try parsley, basil, mint, rosemary, tarragon, oregano, coriander, chives, dill, or thyme?

❶ OIL OR FAT BASE

GROUNDNUT OIL
HEMP SEED OIL
COCONUT OIL
RAPESEED OIL
SUNFLOWER OIL
EXTRA VIRGIN OLIVE OIL
SOURED CREAM
MAYONNAISE
GREEK YOGURT
TAHINI

3 PARTS

½ PART

CHILLI FLAKES

CITRUS ZEST
lemon, lime, grapefruit, orange

SUNDRIED TOMATOES
finely chopped

OLIVES
finely chopped

TOMATOES
finely chopped

❹ VEG, FRUIT, AND SEASONINGS

FRESH OR DRIED HERBS
finely chopped

JALAPEÑOS
finely sliced

BERRIES OR BERRY COULIS
raspberries, blackberries, blueberries, strawberries

MANGO
peeled, stone removed, and finely chopped

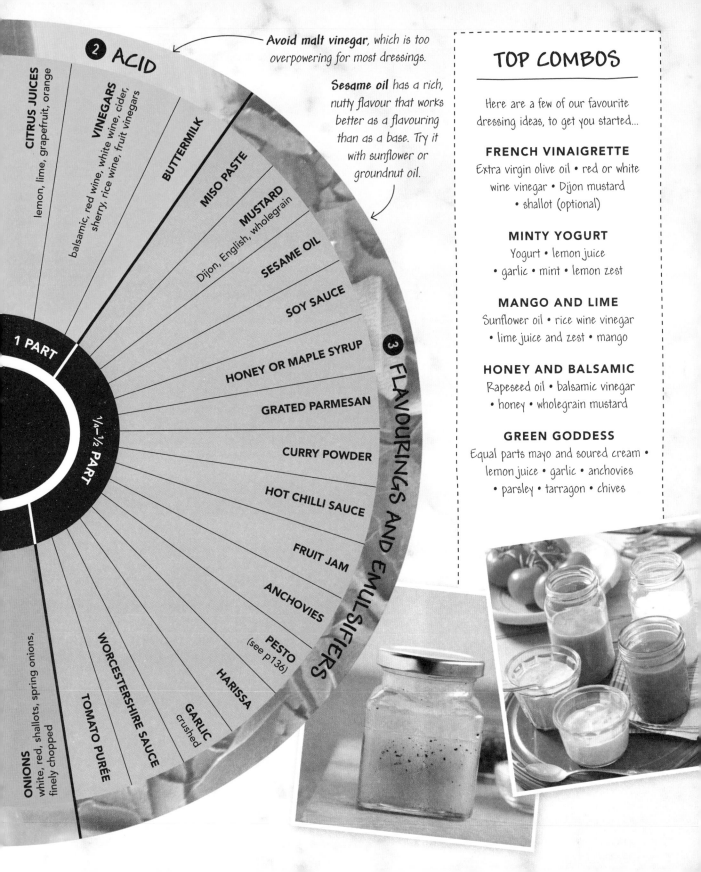

② ACID

1 PART

¼–½ PART

CITRUS JUICES
lemon, lime, grapefruit, orange

VINEGARS
balsamic, red wine, white wine, cider, sherry, rice wine, fruit vinegars

BUTTERMILK

MISO PASTE

MUSTARD
Dijon, English, wholegrain

SESAME OIL

SOY SAUCE

HONEY OR MAPLE SYRUP

GRATED PARMESAN

CURRY POWDER

HOT CHILLI SAUCE

FRUIT JAM

ANCHOVIES

PESTO
(see p136)

GARLIC
crushed

HARISSA

WORCESTERSHIRE SAUCE

TOMATO PURÉE

ONIONS
white, red, shallots, spring onions, finely chopped

③ FLAVOURINGS AND EMULSIFIERS

Avoid malt vinegar, which is too overpowering for most dressings.

Sesame oil has a rich, nutty flavour that works better as a flavouring than as a base. Try it with sunflower or groundnut oil.

TOP COMBOS

Here are a few of our favourite dressing ideas, to get you started...

FRENCH VINAIGRETTE
Extra virgin olive oil • red or white wine vinegar • Dijon mustard • shallot (optional)

MINTY YOGURT
Yogurt • lemon juice • garlic • mint • lemon zest

MANGO AND LIME
Sunflower oil • rice wine vinegar • lime juice and zest • mango

HONEY AND BALSAMIC
Rapeseed oil • balsamic vinegar • honey • wholegrain mustard

GREEN GODDESS
Equal parts mayo and soured cream • lemon juice • garlic • anchovies • parsley • tarragon • chives

WALDORF SALAD

Created at the Waldorf Astoria Hotel in New York, this creamy and crunchy salad has been a favourite for over 100 years. It goes well with grilled chicken if you need something a bit more filling.

SERVES 4 • **READY IN** 15 mins

INGREDIENTS

- 2 large apples
- 4 celery sticks, thinly sliced
- 25 red seedless grapes, halved
- 2 tbsp toasted and crushed walnuts
- 60g (2oz) mayonnaise
- juice of 1 lemon
- salt and freshly ground black pepper
- 2 hearts of Romaine lettuce

❶ DICE THE APPLES

Remove the cores of the apples using a corer. Then, using a sharp knife, cut the apples into slices of an even thickness. Stack the slices, a few at a time, and cut lengthways through the pile and then crossways, making equal-sized cubes.

❷ DRESS AND TOSS THE SALAD

Put the apples, celery, grapes, and walnuts in a bowl. Add the mayonnaise and lemon juice and toss well to combine. Season with salt and pepper to taste.

❸ ADD LETTUCE AND SERVE

Roughly chop the lettuce and divide between 4 plates. Serve the fruit and nut mixture on each bed of lettuce with a squeeze of lemon.

 **PLAN OF ACTION!** ❶ **DICE APPLES** → ❷ **DRESS AND TOSS SALAD** → ❸ **ADD LETTUCE AND SERVE**

TOMATO, MOZZARELLA, AND RED ONION SALAD

10 MINS OR LESS!

Versatile and easy to prepare, this simple salad bursts with vibrant colours and delicious Italian flavours. You can pull this together in minutes – serve it with ciabatta to mop up the juices, if you like.

SERVES 4 • **READY IN** 10 mins

INGREDIENTS

- 8 ripe plum tomatoes, sliced
- 6 cherry tomatoes, halved
- 1 small red onion, peeled and sliced
- handful of basil leaves, torn
- extra virgin olive oil, to drizzle
- salt and freshly ground black pepper
- 2 handfuls of wild rocket leaves
- balsamic vinegar, to drizzle
- 2 balls of mozzarella, torn into pieces

1 DRESS THE INGREDIENTS

Place the tomatoes, onion, and half of the basil leaves in a bowl. Drizzle over plenty of olive oil, season with salt and pepper, and toss through.

2 COMBINE, SEASON, AND SERVE

Arrange the rocket leaves on a serving platter and drizzle over a little oil and balsamic vinegar. Season and spoon over the tomato and basil mixture. Add the torn mozzarella. Scatter over the remaining basil leaves, and drizzle again with a little oil and balsamic vinegar. Serve immediately.

Why not toss this salad through cooked pasta with some garlic oil for a simple summery lunch? Add the rocket at the end to prevent it from wilting.

PLAN OF ACTION!   **1 DRESS INGREDIENTS** → **2 COMBINE AND SERVE**

JEWELLED COUSCOUS IN A JIFFY

PLAN OF ACTION!

A stylish Middle Eastern–inspired salad that you can bring together without any cooking at all. It's easy to make this in the evening, then pack the cool couscous mix in a lunchbox for a healthy weekday lunch. It's cheaper and much tastier than a supermarket sandwich.

SERVES 4-6 • **READY IN** 12 mins

1 MAKE THE STOCK

Boil a kettle. Put the couscous into a bowl and drizzle over the ½ tbsp of olive oil. Rub it into the couscous, scatter over the powdered vegetable stock (if using), and mix it in.

2 SOAK THE COUSCOUS

Pour over 525ml (17fl oz) of boiling water (if using powdered stock) or hot vegetable stock, and stir briefly. The liquid should just cover the couscous. Immediately seal with cling film.

3 REST, TEST, AND COOL

Leave for 5 minutes, then test the grains, which should be nearly soft, and all the water soaked in. Fork over the couscous and leave it to cool, forking it occasionally to separate the grains.

4 TOAST THE PINE NUTS

Meanwhile dry-fry the pine nuts in a non-stick frying pan over a medium heat, stirring, until they colour. Be careful, as they can burn quickly. Set aside to cool.

5 MIX IT ALL UP

Toss together the cooled couscous, pine nuts, apricots, and coriander. Mix in the extra virgin olive oil and lemon juice and season to taste. Scatter over the pomegranate seeds to serve.

INGREDIENTS

300g (10oz) couscous

1½ tbsp olive oil

1 tbsp powdered vegetable stock or 525ml (17fl oz) hot vegetable stock

50g (1¾oz) pine nuts

100g (3½oz) dried apricots, finely chopped

large handful of coriander leaves, finely chopped

salt and freshly ground black pepper

4½ tbsp extra virgin olive oil

juice of 1 large lemon

2 or 3 tbsp pomegranate seeds, to serve

INGREDIENTS

350g (12oz) fillet steak, or thick rump steak

200g (7oz) rice vermicelli or mung bean noodles

250g (9oz) green papaya or green mango, peeled, deseeded, and cut into matchsticks or coarsely grated

4 tbsp roasted unsalted peanuts, coarsely chopped

FOR THE DRESSING

1 tsp lemongrass purée

1 tsp finely grated fresh root ginger

2 tbsp chopped coriander

2 tbsp Vietnamese nuoc mam or Thai fish sauce

2 tbsp chopped mint

juice of 2 limes

1 tsp brown sugar

2 fresh red chillies, deseeded and finely chopped

 PLAN OF ACTION!

1 GRILL BEEF → **2** SOAK NOODLES → **3** MAKE DRESSING

TOSS
AND SERVE

GREEN PAPAYA, BEEF, AND NOODLE SALAD

A vibrant, Vietnamese-inspired noodle salad, this meal makes for a refreshing lunch. Green papayas are under-ripe fruit that feature in many Southeast Asian salads – if you can't find papaya, green mango works just as well.

SERVES 4 • **READY IN** 20 mins, plus resting

1 TRIM AND GRILL THE BEEF

Preheat the grill to high. Trim any fat from the steak and grill for 3–4 minutes on each side, or until browned but still pink in the centre. Set aside for at least 15 minutes before slicing into thin strips.

2 SOAK THE NOODLES

Soak the vermicelli, or noodles, in boiling water until softened, or as directed on the packet. Drain, rinse in cold water, then cut into manageable lengths with kitchen scissors. Set aside.

3 MAKE THE DRESSING

Mix together the lemongrass, ginger, coriander, fish sauce, mint, lime juice, sugar, and chillies.

4 TOSS TOGETHER AND SERVE

Pile the noodles, papaya, and steak into a serving dish and add the dressing. Toss lightly together and scatter with peanuts before serving.

TIP – If you want, you can grill the steak several hours in advance, and slice it just before adding to the salad.

This salad appears in many variations across Vietnam, Thailand, and Cambodia. Why not try eating it Thai-style? Use grilled chicken in place of the beef, and sticky white rice instead of noodles.

SPICY ASIAN CHICKEN SALAD

This colourful salad is tasty as well as healthy, and requires very little cooking. You can reserve some of the salad, undressed, for tomorrow's lunch; toss with the dressing at the last minute to prevent wilting.

SERVES 4–6 • **READY IN** 20 mins

INGREDIENTS

- 400g (14oz) skinless boneless chicken breasts
- salt
- chicken stock, if using
- 4 tbsp lime juice (approx. 2 limes)
- 4 tsp Thai fish sauce
- 1 tbsp caster sugar
- pinch of chilli flakes (optional)
- 1 little gem lettuce, shredded
- 100g (3½oz) beansprouts
- 1 large carrot, shaved using a vegetable peeler
- 15cm (6in) piece of cucumber, deseeded and finely sliced
- ½ red pepper, finely sliced
- ½ yellow pepper, finely sliced
- approx. 15 cherry tomatoes, halved
- small handful of mint leaves, chopped
- small handful of coriander leaves, chopped
- 50g (1¾oz) salted peanuts, chopped (optional)

❶ POACH THE CHICKEN

Poach the chicken in a large saucepan in plenty of simmering salted water or chicken stock, if using, for 7–10 minutes, depending on the thickness, until cooked through. Let cool, then thinly slice.

❷ MAKE THE DRESSING

Whisk the lime juice, fish sauce, sugar, a pinch of salt, and the chilli flakes, if using, together until the sugar dissolves.

❸ TOSS TOGETHER AND SERVE

Mix together the salad vegetables, most of the herbs, and the chicken. Mix in the dressing and scatter with the remaining herbs and the peanuts, if using, to serve.

TIP – To save time, prepare the vegetables while the chicken is poaching. To speed-cut cherry tomatoes, place several on a small plate, invert a second small plate on top, and, holding the top plate in place, use a sharp knife to slice between the plates and through the tomatoes, making sure you cut away from yourself.

 PLAN OF ACTION!   **① POACH CHICKEN** → **② MAKE DRESSING** → **③ TOSS AND SERVE**

BULGUR WHEAT WITH MIXED PEPPERS AND GOAT'S CHEESE

Sweet, crunchy peppers and creamy goat's cheese are a winning combination. Bulgur wheat is a great staple for your cupboard – it's a source of fibre and protein, and very easy to prepare.

SERVES 4 • **READY IN** 15 mins

INGREDIENTS

- 250g (9oz) fine bulgur wheat
- 300ml (10fl oz) hot vegetable stock
- salt and freshly ground black pepper
- 1 bunch of spring onions, finely chopped
- 1 orange pepper, deseeded and diced
- 1 yellow pepper, deseeded and diced
- pinch of mild paprika
- handful of fresh mint leaves, finely chopped
- juice of 1 lemon
- 125g (4½oz) soft goat's cheese, crumbled
- extra virgin olive oil, for drizzling

1 SOAK THE BULGUR WHEAT
Put the bulgur wheat in a large bowl, and pour over enough stock just to cover the bulgur. Leave to stand for 10 minutes, then stir with a fork to fluff up the grains. Season with salt and pepper.

2 ADD THE VEG AND CHEESE
Add the spring onions, orange and yellow peppers, paprika, mint, and lemon juice, and stir well. Taste, and season again if needed. To serve, top with the goat's cheese and a generous drizzle of olive oil.

You could use
couscous instead of bulgur wheat and feta instead of goat's cheese, if you like. For the couscous, pour over enough hot stock just to cover the couscous, then cover the bowl with cling film and leave for 5 minutes before fluffing up with a fork.

PLAN OF ACTION!

1
SOAK BULGUR WHEAT

2
ADD VEG AND CHEESE

BEAN BURGERS

These bean burgers are a tasty, low-fat alternative to the traditional beef burger, and can be put together in no time! Omit the anchovies to make them vegetarian.

MAKES 6 • **READY IN** 20 mins

SPECIAL EQUIPMENT Food processor

- 400g can aduki beans, drained and rinsed
- 400g can chickpeas, drained and rinsed
- 1 onion, roughly chopped
- 6 salted anchovies in olive oil, drained
- 1 tbsp wholegrain mustard
- salt and freshly ground black pepper
- 2 eggs

- 2–3 tbsp plain flour, plus extra for dusting
- 2–3 tbsp vegetable or sunflower oil, for frying

TO SERVE

- 2 burger buns, toasted
- crisp lettuce, such as little gem
- tomato ketchup

PREPARE THE BEANS

1 RINSE

chickpeas

aduki beans

COLANDER

Drain and rinse the beans in a colander.

2 PULSE BEANS

Give the chickpeas and aduki beans a quick whizz or two until they're broken up.

FOOD PROCESSOR

If you don't have a food processor, you can use a potato masher to crush the beans to a rough paste before stirring in the remaining ingredients. Make sure you chop the anchovies and whisk the eggs before adding.

ADD THE OTHER INGREDIENTS

3 ADD FLAVOURINGS

onions anchovies mustard

Pulse again ...

4 ADD EGGS

eggs salt pepper

... and again ...

5 ADD FLOUR

... and again!

FORM AND FRY

6 FORM

Form into patties.

7 FRY

Heat the oil and fry in batches of 2 or 3 over a medium heat for 3–4 minutes on each side, or until golden.

ASSEMBLE THE BURGERS

8 STACK

bun

tomato ketchup

bean burger

lettuce

bun

TUNA AND ARTICHOKE SALAD

A hearty meal-in-one salad, this dish is enhanced by a few storecupboard ingredients and some fresh green beans. It's packed with flavour and pretty enough to share! Prepare ahead for a tasty weekday packed lunch.

SERVES 4 • **READY IN** 20 mins

1 BOIL THE PASTA AND BEANS

Bring a large pan of water to the boil and cook the pasta according to the packet instructions, adding the green beans 4–5 minutes before the end of the cooking time. Drain and rinse under cold running water until the pasta is cold. Drain well and place in a serving dish. Add the tuna, cannellini beans, sun-dried tomatoes, and artichokes and stir well.

2 MAKE THE DRESSING

Place 3 tablespoons of the oil from the sun-dried tomatoes and 3 tablespoons of the oil from the drained artichokes in a small jug. Stir in the lemon zest and juice, mustard, and seasoning.

3 DRESS THE SALAD

Pour the lemon-mustard dressing over the pasta. Add the herbs and toss well to coat. Cover and chill until ready to serve.

TIP – Save any remaining oil from the sun-dried tomatoes and artichokes. As well as being delicious in salad dressings, the oils add extra flavour when frying vegetables.

For a vegetarian version, omit the tuna and add a 250g jar of roasted pepper strips instead, and a handful of rinsed capers or green olives.

INGREDIENTS

220g (7¾oz) quick-cook pasta shapes

100g (3½oz) fine green beans, topped, tailed, and halved

200g can of tuna in spring water, drained and flaked

400g can of cannellini beans, drained and rinsed

10 sun-dried tomatoes in oil, drained and roughly chopped (oil reserved)

250g jar artichoke hearts in oil, drained (oil reserved)

finely grated zest and juice of 1 lemon

1 tsp wholegrain mustard

salt and freshly ground black pepper

3 tbsp chopped flat-leaf parsley leaves

leaves from 3 sprigs of basil, torn

DO-IT-YOURSELF SUSHI

TO MAKE THE SUSHI RICE...

1 Rinse 200g (7oz) of shari or sushi rice in running water.

2 Add to a saucepan with 240ml (8fl oz) of water.

3 Bring to a boil, stir, lower the heat to medium, then cover.

4 Leave to simmer for 6–8 minutes, or until the water has been absorbed.

5 Transfer the cooked rice to a mixing bowl.

6 Mix in 120ml (4fl oz) rice vinegar, 1 tbsp sugar, and a pinch of salt.

TO MAKE THE SUSHI ROLLS...

1 Place a sheet of nori (seaweed) on a bamboo mat. Cover the nori in a 5mm (¼in) layer of cooled sushi rice, pressing it down with your fingertips. Leave uncovered a 1cm (½in) strip along the top of the nori, furthest away from you.

2 Add a layer of filling in a strip along the bottom of the nori, closest to you.

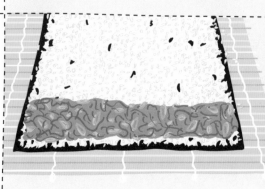

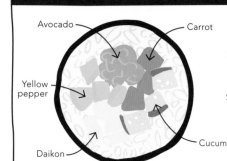

Avocado — Carrot

Yellow pepper

Daikon — Cucumber

GARDEN ROLL

Fill with 1 **avocado**, sliced, 50g (1³/₄oz) each of **carrot** and **cucumber** matchsticks, 1 **yellow pepper**, finely chopped, and 1 **daikon**, peeled and thinly sliced.

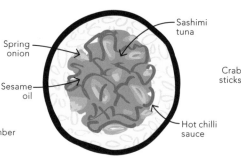

Sashimi tuna

Spring onion

Sesame oil

Hot chilli sauce

SPICY TUNA ROLL

Fill with 75g (2¹/₂oz) fresh **sashimi tuna**, finely chopped, combined with 1 tbsp **hot chilli sauce**, a dash of **sesame oil**, and 1 tbsp **spring onion**, sliced.

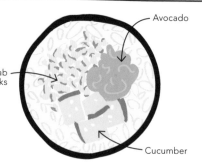

Avocado

Crab sticks

Cucumber

CALIFORNIA ROLL

Fill with 1 **avocado**, sliced, 50g (1³/₄oz) **cucumber** cut into matchsticks, and 2 **crab sticks**, shredded.

These delicious sushi rolls are surprisingly quick and easy to make – and they're ideal for lunch on the go. Follow the basic rice and rolling technique, then choose from the fillings at the bottom of the page. If you prepare the filling ingredients while the rice is cooking, the sushi will be ready in 20 minutes. Makes 1 good serving.

3 Tightly roll the bamboo mat, starting from the end closest to you. Tuck in the edge of the nori, but lift the mat up as you roll it forward. Wet the uncovered end of the nori with rice wine vinegar and, as you finish the roll, press to seal.

TO SERVE...

Serve the sushi rolls with **pickled ginger**, and **soy sauce** and **wasabi** to dip.

You can buy pre-prepared **pickled ginger**, but if you have a little extra time it's fun to make your own. Simply toss 225g (8oz) **young root ginger**, peeled and finely sliced, with 1 tbsp **salt**. Leave for 30 minutes. Mix together 240ml (8fl oz) **rice vinegar** and 50g (1³/₄oz) **sugar**. Bring to a boil, then pour over the salted ginger. Leave to cool before serving, or refrigerate for up to two weeks.

4 Trim the edges of the roll so they are straight and neat, then slice the roll into 8 equal pieces.

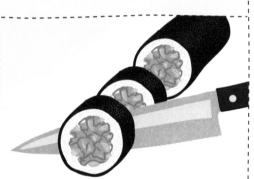

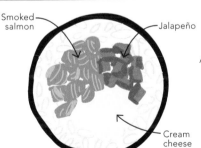

Smoked salmon — Jalapeño — Cream cheese

PHILADELPHIA ROLL
Fill with 1 **jalapeño** or other mild green chilli pepper, deseeded and finely chopped, 3 tbsp **cream cheese**, and 50g (1³/₄oz) **smoked salmon**.

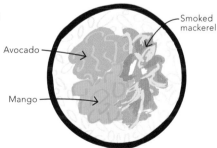

Avocado — Smoked mackerel — Mango

SMOKED MACKEREL ROLL
Fill with 75g (2¹/₂oz) **smoked mackerel**, shredded, 50g (1³/₄oz) **fresh mango**, sliced, and 1 **avocado**, sliced.

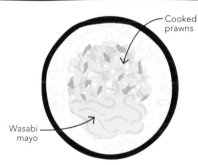

Cooked prawns — Wasabi mayo

WASABI PRAWN ROLL
Fill with 75g (2¹/₂oz) **cooked prawns**, chopped, and 3 tbsp **wasabi mayo** (make by combining mayonnaise with a little wasabi paste, to taste).

SQUASH FRITTATA

This easy-to-prepare frittata is packed with the goodness of butternut squash and spinach, and makes for a quick, delicious, and wholesome meal.

SERVES 2 • **READY IN** 20–30 mins

- 1 small butternut squash, about 500g (1lb 2oz), deseeded and diced
- 2 tbsp olive oil
- knob of butter
- 1 small onion, diced
- 200g (7oz) spinach
- 125g (4½oz) soft goat's cheese
- 4 pieces of semi-dried tomatoes in oil, drained and cut into small pieces
- 2 tbsp grated Parmesan cheese
- grated nutmeg
- 2 tbsp chopped tarragon
- 6 eggs, beaten
- salt and freshly ground black pepper

COOK THE FILLING

1 BLANCH

SAUCEPAN

butternut squash

boiling water

Blanch (briefly boil) the butternut squash for 2–4 minutes, until slightly softened.

2 DRAIN

COLANDER

Thoroughly drain the squash.

3 SOFTEN

WOODEN SPOON

onions

butternut squash

oil and butter

LARGE NON-STICK FRYING PAN

Heat the oil and butter, add the onion, and cook for 3 minutes. Then add the squash and cook for 2 minutes.

4 WILT

spinach

WHILE THE SPINACH IS SIMMERING, SEASON THE BEATEN EGGS AND PREHEAT THE GRILL TO ITS HIGHEST SETTING.

If you like, use Swiss chard or pak choi in place of the spinach.

Add the spinach and cook for 2 minutes to wilt. Simmer for 1–2 minutes more to drive off any liquid, stirring gently.

5 ADD FLAVOURINGS

goat's cheese   semi-dried tomatoes   tarragon   nutmeg   Parmesan

Add the goat's cheese and tomatoes and spread them out evenly. Sprinkle over the Parmesan, nutmeg, and tarragon.

COOK THE EGGS THEN GRILL

Lift and stir the eggs.

FRYING PAN LID

6 ADD EGGS

Cook the eggs until just beginning to set, then cover and cook for 5 more minutes.

Remove the lid, transfer the pan to the grill, and cook for 3–4 minutes to brown the top. Cut into wedges and serve.

7 GRILL

QUICK FRITTATA

A fancy version of cheesy scrambled eggs with tomato, this dish, known as "kayiana" in Greek cuisine, is the ultimate comfort food – ideal for a warming, filling lunch ready in no time.

SERVES 4-5 • **READY IN** 20 mins

INGREDIENTS

- 4 tbsp olive oil
- 2 large ripe, firm tomatoes, thickly sliced
- 1 garlic clove, chopped
- 100g (3½oz) mozzarella or taleggio cheese, diced
- 6 large eggs
- 1 tbsp finely chopped dill
- salt and freshly ground black pepper

① COOK THE TOMATOES

Heat the oil in a small frying pan. Spread the tomato slices in an even layer over the surface and sprinkle over the garlic. Cook over a gentle heat until the tomatoes are soft and slightly dry. Top the tomatoes with the cheese and cook until it has melted slightly.

② PREPARE THE EGGS

While the tomatoes and cheese are cooking, place the eggs and dill in a large bowl. Season and beat until well combined. Pour the egg mixture over the tomatoes and melted cheese and increase the heat to medium. Cover partially and cook until the top is beginning to set.

③ FLIP AND FINISH

Place a large plate over the pan and flip it over to transfer the frittata. Reduce the heat to low and return the frittata to the pan, uncooked side up. Cook for a further 2–3 minutes, or until the underneath is golden brown and set. Remove from the heat. Slice the frittata into wedges, and serve immediately.

 **PLAN OF ACTION!**   **① COOK TOMATOES** → **② PREPARE EGGS** → **③ FLIP AND FINISH**

BROAD BEAN TORTILLA

This Spanish recipe combines eggs with lightly fried broad beans – instead of the usual potatoes – for a flavoursome yet quick lunch. You could even cut it into bite-sized pieces to serve as tapas.

SERVES 4-6 • **READY IN** 20 mins

INGREDIENTS

- 4 tbsp olive oil
- 500g (1lb 2oz) broad beans, shelled
- 2 tbsp white wine or dry sherry
- 4 large eggs
- 1 tsp fresh marjoram leaves
- salt and freshly ground black pepper

❶ FRY THE BEANS

Heat 1 tablespoon of the oil in a small frying pan. Remove and discard any wrinkled skins from the beans, then add the beans to the pan and cook for 1 minute, turning them over once. Add the wine, or sherry, stir to mix, and cook until the alcohol evaporates. Reduce the heat to a simmer, cover, and cook for 5–6 minutes, or until the beans are just soft and the liquid has almost evaporated. Remove from the heat and leave to cool.

❷ PREPARE THE EGGS

Place the eggs and marjoram leaves in a large bowl. Season to taste and beat well to combine. Then add the bean mixture to the bowl and stir well to mix.

❸ COOK THE TORTILLA

Heat the remaining oil in the pan. Pour in the egg and bean mixture and spread it out in an even layer. Cook the tortilla over a gentle heat, neatening the edges with a spatula, until the top is beginning to set and the underneath is golden brown.

❹ FLIP AND FINISH

Flip the tortilla over (see step 3, opposite) and cook for a further 2–3 minutes, or until the tortilla is firm but still juicy in the middle. Serve warm or cool.

 ❶ FRY BEANS → ❷ PREPARE EGGS → ❸ COOK TORTILLA → ❹ FLIP AND FINISH

UPCYCLED LEFTOVERS

CHICKEN

Cooked chicken is a great addition to all sorts of meals; simply shred it into small pieces to make it go further before adding to sandwiches, wraps, or salads. Keep cooled cooked chicken, covered, in the fridge for up to 3 days.

CHICKEN TACOS
Toss 100g (3½oz) shredded chicken with a dash of cider vinegar and a pinch each of chilli flakes and smoked paprika. Layer in taco shells with salsa and guacamole (see p146), and thinly sliced red onions.

OR

CHICKEN SOUP
Fry 1 onion (chopped), ½ stick celery (chopped), 1 carrot (diced) in butter until they begin to soften. Stir in 1 tbsp plain flour and cook for 2 minutes. Add 250ml (16fl oz) chicken stock and simmer for 10 minutes, until the vegetables are tender. Add 100g (3½oz) cooked, shredded chicken and cook until heated through. Season to taste and serve scattered with chopped parsley.

OR

Barbecue chicken sandwich (p68) • Chicken and apple salad pitta pocket (p78) • Shredded chicken in yellow curry sauce pitta pocket (p79) • Asian noodle salad (p88) • Spicy Asian chicken salad (p98) • Red curry in a hurry (p134)

BREAD

Tear leftover bread, toast it, and add it to a panzanella or an eggy casserole. Breadcrumbs are also a great staple – they act as a binding agent in meatballs, sausages, and burgers, and make a crispy coating or crust for baked and fried foods.

PANZANELLA
Toss 2 slices of stale bread (cut into bite-sized pieces), 100g (3½oz) ripe tomatoes (chopped), ½ red onion (thinly sliced), and ¼ cucumber (chopped) with 1 tsp red wine vinegar and 3 tsp extra virgin olive oil, and season to taste. Set aside for half an hour, before serving with a small handful each of chopped parsley and torn basil scattered over.

OR

EASY BREADCRUMBS
Freeze slices of bread and grate using a cheese grater.

OR

For whole pieces or slices:
Strawberry-stuffed French toast (p40) • Sweet potato soup (pp82–3 – for the croutons) • The Bruschetta Bar (pp180–1)
For breadcrumbs:
Chicken schnitzel (pp118–19) • Classic beef burgers (p121) • Harissa-spiced lamb chops (pp206–7)

Transforming your leftovers into tasty new meals is a quick and easy way to save both time and money on tomorrow's lunch or dinner. It can be a good idea to deliberately cook more of the ingredients below than you need, as these staples are particularly versatile. The quantities below are for 1 serving.

RICE

Cool any leftover rice as soon as possible after cooking, keep it in the fridge, and use it within 24 hours. If reheating, ensure that it's steaming hot throughout before serving.

MEXICAN GREEN RICE

Blend a handful each of coriander and parsley, fresh chilli (to taste), 1 onion, and 1 garlic clove to a paste in a food processor or blender. Combine with 200g (7oz) cooked rice. To serve, roll in tortillas with shredded cooked chicken and chilli sauce.

FRIED RICE

Stir-fry 200g (7oz) cooked rice in 1 tbsp sesame oil in a wok over a medium-high heat until heated through. Add 2 eggs (beaten) and continue to stir-fry until the egg is set. Stir through a handful of cooked peas and a bunch of finely chopped spring onions. Season, and serve straight away.

Sopa al cuatro de hora (p84) • Stir-fry in no time (pp 124–5) • Arancini (p131) • Simple stuffed vegetables (pp132–3)

POTATOES

Boiled, mashed, or baked – potatoes are a versatile leftover ingredient perfect for second-day meals. Cooked potatoes are best re-used within 3 days.

CHEAT'S PIEROGI

Mix 125g (4½oz) mashed cooked potato with 125g (4½oz) soft cheese. Fold into gyoza or wonton skins (for folding technique, see pp184–5). Boil the dumplings in a large pot of water for 2–3 minutes before removing with a slotted spoon. Serve immediately with soured cream, chopped parsley, and onions fried in butter.

BUBBLE AND SQUEAK

Mix 125g (4½oz) mashed cooked potato with a large handful of cooked, chopped cabbage (kale or greens work just as well). Form into patties or shape into 1 large cake to fit the frying pan. Fry in melted butter for about 3 minutes on each side, or until crispy and golden brown.

Squash frittata (pp106–107, using potato instead of the butternut squash) • Potato, pancetta, and red onion hash (p62)

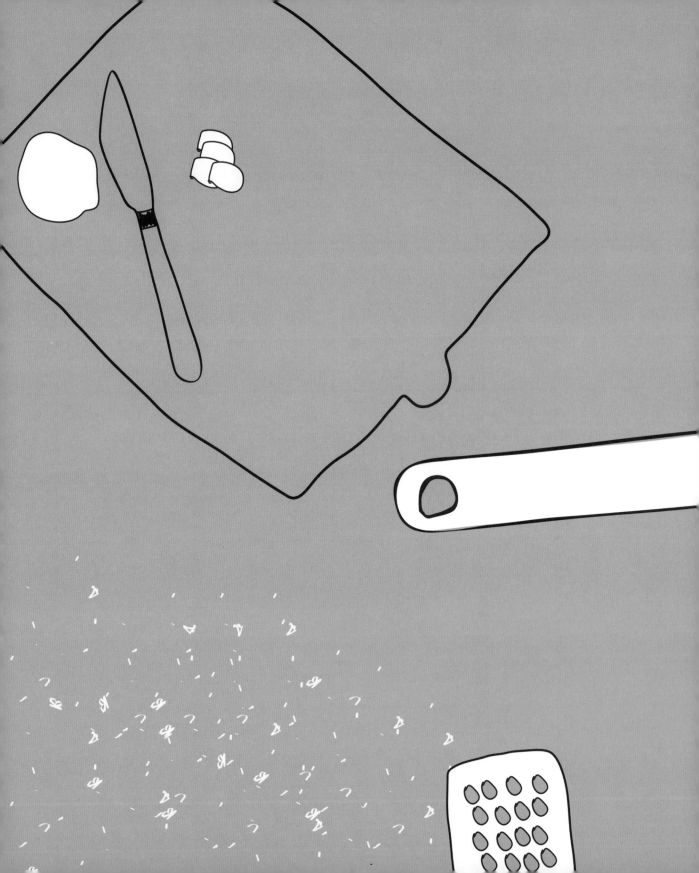

QUICK WEEK-NIGHT
SUPPERS

INGREDIENTS

salt and freshly ground black pepper

550g (1¼lb) new potatoes, well scrubbed and chopped into bite-sized chunks

200g (7oz) hot-smoked mackerel fillets, skinned

60g (2oz) baby salad leaves

2 tbsp chopped dill

2 tbsp chopped chives

200g (7oz) cooked beetroot (not in vinegar), roughly chopped

baguette, to serve

FOR THE DRESSING
4 tbsp extra virgin olive oil
juice of 1 lemon
1 tsp wholegrain mustard
1 tsp clear honey
1 garlic clove, finely chopped

→ **4**
DRESS AND SERVE

HERBED MACKEREL SALAD

Throw together this fragrant salad for a light supper packed with flavour – and then mop up the delicious dressing with a crispy baguette. Smoked mackerel is great to have in the fridge as it's inexpensive and high in protein.

SERVES 4 • **READY IN** 20 mins

① COOK THE POTATOES

Bring a large pan of salted water to the boil, add the potato chunks, and cook for 10–15 minutes, or until tender. Drain and set aside.

② PREPARE THE MACKEREL

Meanwhile, break the mackerel into bite-sized pieces, removing any bones you find as you go, and place in a large serving bowl. Add the salad leaves and herbs, and gently toss together.

③ MAKE THE DRESSING

Place the dressing ingredients in a small jug, season, and whisk together with a fork.

④ DRESS, COMBINE, AND SERVE

Add the warm potatoes to the serving bowl, pour over the dressing, and stir gently. Add the beetroot and serve straight away with the baguette.

TIP – Roll the lemon across the worktop before squeezing it. You'll get lots more juice from the fruit without having to work as hard.

CHICKEN SALAD WITH RADICCHIO AND ASPARAGUS

This French "salade tiède", or warm salad, is quick to cook and easy to assemble. Crunchy lettuce and garlicky chicken with a punchy dressing makes for a healthy supper you can knock together in minutes.

SERVES 4 • READY IN 15 MINUTES

- -

1 COOK THE CHICKEN

Heat 2 tablespoons of the oil in a large non-stick frying pan over a medium-high heat. Add the chicken and garlic and fry, stirring, for 5–7 minutes, or until the chicken is tender and cooked through. Stir in the roasted red peppers, and season to taste with salt and pepper.

2 COMBINE WITH THE RADICCHIO

Meanwhile, put the radicchio leaves in a large serving bowl. Remove the chicken from the pan, using a slotted spoon, and place in the bowl with the radicchio.

3 FRY THE ASPARAGUS

Add the asparagus to the fat remaining in the pan and fry, stirring constantly, for 1–2 minutes, or until just tender. Transfer to the bowl with the chicken.

4 DRESS, TOSS, AND EAT

Whisk together the remaining 2 tablespoons of the oil, the vinegar and sugar, then pour into the pan and stir over a high heat until well combined. Pour this dressing over the salad and toss quickly so that all the ingredients are well mixed and coated with the dressing. Serve straight away.

You can substitute another vinegar for raspberry; try red wine or cider vinegar.

1 COOK CHICKEN → **2** ADD TO RADICCHIO → **3** FRY ASPARAGUS → **4** DRESS AND EAT

INGREDIENTS

4 tbsp extra virgin olive oil

4 chicken breasts, about 150g (5½oz) each, cut into thin strips

1 garlic clove, finely chopped

60g (2oz) roasted red peppers, thinly sliced

salt and freshly ground black pepper

1 small head of radicchio, torn into small pieces

250g (9oz) asparagus spears, each trimmed and cut into 3 pieces

2 tbsp raspberry vinegar

½ tsp sugar

CHICKEN SCHNITZEL

This zesty breaded chicken can be ready in no time!
Serve with a green salad and potato wedges or boiled
baby potatoes for a speedy week-night supper.

SERVES 2 • **READY IN** 15 mins

- 2 large skinless chicken breast fillets
- salt and freshly ground black pepper
- 125g (4½oz) fresh breadcrumbs
- grated zest of 1 lemon
- 1 tbsp plain flour

- 1 egg, lightly beaten
- 1 tbsp olive oil

FOR THE SAUCE
- 4–6 fresh sage leaves, finely chopped
- juice of 1 lemon

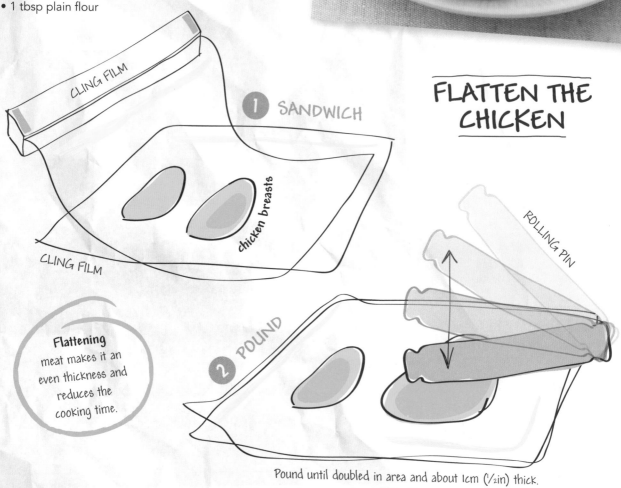

CLING FILM

1 SANDWICH

chicken breasts

CLING FILM

FLATTEN THE CHICKEN

ROLLING PIN

Flattening meat makes it an even thickness and reduces the cooking time.

2 POUND

Pound until doubled in area and about 1cm (½in) thick.

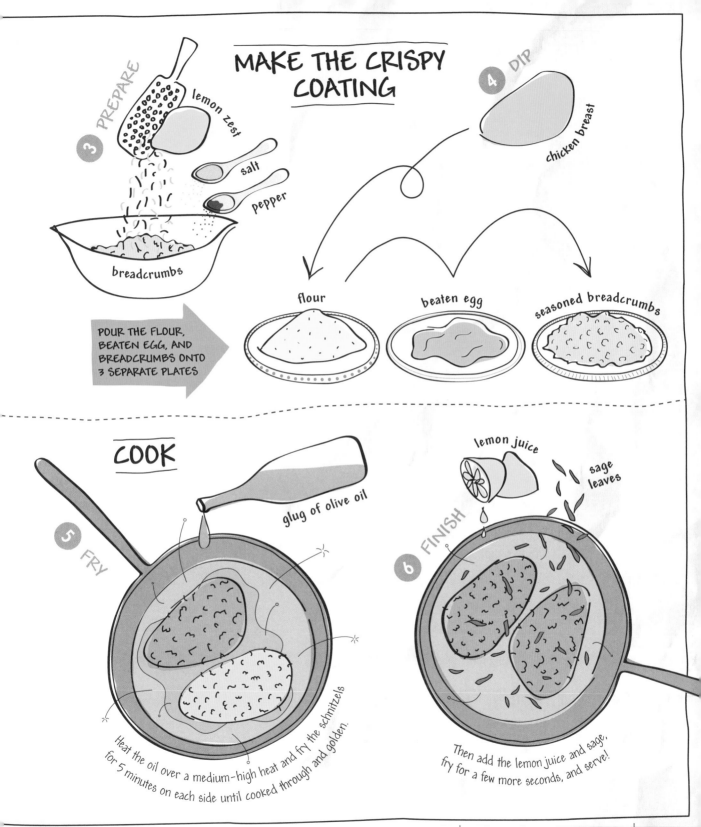

MAKE THE CRISPY COATING

3 PREPARE

lemon zest

salt

pepper

breadcrumbs

4 DIP

chicken breast

POUR THE FLOUR, BEATEN EGG, AND BREADCRUMBS ONTO 3 SEPARATE PLATES

flour

beaten egg

seasoned breadcrumbs

COOK

5 FRY

glug of olive oil

Heat the oil over a medium-high heat and fry the schnitzels for 5 minutes on each side until cooked through and golden.

6 FINISH

lemon juice

sage leaves

Then add the lemon juice and sage, fry for a few more seconds, and serve!

CHICKEN ESCALOPES WITH LEMON SAUCE

An escalope is a piece of meat, in this case chicken, that is pounded to make it thinner; this speeds up the cooking process and makes it more tender. Serve with steamed spring vegetables and new potatoes.

SERVES 4 • READY IN 20 mins

INGREDIENTS

- 4 skinless boneless chicken breasts
- 1 tbsp olive oil
- salt and freshly ground black pepper
- 3 tbsp plain flour
- 1 tbsp butter
- 250ml (9fl oz) chicken stock
- juice of ½ lemon
- 4 heaped tbsp crème fraîche
- 1 tbsp finely chopped thyme leaves
- ½ tsp caster sugar

1 FLATTEN THE CHICKEN
Preheat the oven to 150°C (300°F/Gas 2). Pound each chicken breast with the round side of a rolling pin until 1cm (½in) thick all over.

2 FRY THE ESCALOPES
Heat the oil in a large, heavy-based frying pan. Season just 2 tablespoons of the flour with salt and pepper. Dust the chicken with the flour, shaking off any excess. Fry the chicken for 5 minutes on each side over a medium heat, until cooked through and golden. Transfer the cooked escalopes to a baking dish and pop in the oven to keep warm.

3 MAKE THE SAUCE
Wipe the frying pan clean with kitchen paper. Melt the butter in the pan and scatter over the remaining 1 tablespoon of flour, whisking over a medium heat for 1 minute. Gradually add the stock and lemon juice, whisking constantly, and bring to a boil.

4 THICKEN SAUCE AND SERVE WITH CHICKEN
Add the crème fraîche, thyme, and sugar, and season with salt and pepper. Cook the sauce for 5 minutes, until thick and glossy, whisking constantly with a balloon whisk. Remove the chicken from the oven, spoon out the juices, and add them to the sauce. Slice the chicken on the diagonal and pour the sauce over to serve.

PLAN OF ACTION! 1 FLATTEN CHICKEN → 2 FRY ESCALOPES → 3 MAKE SAUCE → 4 THICKEN SAUCE AND SERVE

CLASSIC BEEF BURGERS

Homemade beef burgers are always worth the effort – they're simple and satisfying to make, and taste so much better than shop-bought ones. Serve in a bun with salad and relishes.

MAKES 4 • **READY IN** 20 mins, plus chilling

INGREDIENTS

- 400g (14oz) good-quality minced beef
- 50g (1¾oz) fresh white breadcrumbs
- 1 egg yolk
- ½ red onion, finely chopped
- ½ tsp dried mustard powder
- ½ tsp celery salt
- 1 tsp Worcestershire sauce
- freshly ground black pepper
- 2 tbsp olive oil

TO SERVE
- 4 burger buns, halved
- 1 round lettuce, shredded
- 2 tomatoes, thickly sliced
- 1 small red onion, finely sliced
- 1 gherkin, finely sliced
- 4 tbsp spicy tomato relish

1 PREPARE THE BEEF MIX

In a large bowl, mix together all the burger ingredients (except the oil) until they are well combined.

2 SHAPE THE BURGERS

With damp hands (to help stop the mixture sticking to your fingers), divide the mixture into 4 balls and roll each one between your palms until smooth. Pressing down with your palms, flatten each ball out into a large, fat disk to a thickness of 3cm (1¼in), and pat the edges in to tidy them up.

3 CHILL THE BURGERS

Place the burgers on a plate, cover with cling film, and chill for 30 minutes (this will help them to keep their shape during cooking).

4 FRY THE BURGERS

Heat the oil in a large frying pan and fry the burgers for 5–6 minutes on each side, until the meat is springy to the touch and the edges are charred.

5 PREPARE THE BUNS AND SERVE

While the burgers are frying, toast the buns in a dry frying pan over a medium heat until golden. Assemble the burgers and buns with a selection of the listed accompaniments, to your liking.

PLAN OF ACTION!
1 PREPARE BEEF MIX → **2** SHAPE BURGERS → **3** CHILL BURGERS → **4** FRY BURGERS → **5** PREPARE BUNS AND SERVE

THAI-SPICED MEATBALLS WITH PEANUT SAUCE

These fragrant, savoury bites are perfect with a sweet peanut sauce. Serve them with lime juice squeezed over, and white basmati or jasmine rice on the side, for a filling, Thai-inspired dinner.

SERVES 4 • **READY IN** 20 mins

INGREDIENTS

FOR THE MEATBALLS

- 450g (1lb) lean minced beef or pork, or a combination of both
- 1 garlic clove, finely chopped
- 1 tsp lemongrass purée
- 1 tbsp chopped coriander
- 1 tbsp Thai red curry paste
- 1 tbsp lemon juice
- 1 tbsp Thai fish sauce
- 1 egg
- salt and freshly ground black pepper
- rice flour, for dusting
- sunflower oil, for frying
- lime wedges, to garnish

FOR THE PEANUT SAUCE

- 1 tbsp vegetable oil
- 1 tsp Thai red curry paste
- 2 tbsp crunchy peanut butter
- 1 tbsp brown sugar
- 1 tbsp lemon juice
- 250ml (9fl oz) coconut milk

1 MAKE THE PEANUT SAUCE

Heat the oil in a small saucepan, add the curry paste, and fry for 1 minute. Gradually stir in the rest of the ingredients, then bring to the boil. Reduce the heat and simmer for 5 minutes, or until thickened. If it is too thick, stir in a little water.

2 PREPARE THE MIXTURE

Meanwhile, combine the minced meat, garlic, lemongrass, coriander, curry paste, lemon juice, Thai fish sauce, and egg, and season with salt and pepper. Roll the mixture into small walnut-sized balls and dust with the rice flour.

3 FRY THE MEATBALLS

Heat the oil in a frying pan. Fry the meatballs in batches until browned and cooked through.

4 DRAIN AND SERVE

Drain on kitchen paper, then serve hot, with the warm peanut sauce and lime wedges.

 PLAN OF ACTION! → **1 MAKE PEANUT SAUCE** → **2 PREPARE MIXTURE** →  **3 FRY MEATBALLS** →  **4 DRAIN AND SERVE**

DAN DAN NOODLES

The spicy Sichuan classic, named after the carrying pole used by street vendors selling the dish, has been simplified here to include easily available ingredients. Vary the chilli heat levels to your taste.

SERVES 4 • **READY IN** 20 mins

INGREDIENTS

- 300g (10oz) dried Chinese egg noodles
- salt
- 200g (7oz) small broccoli florets
- 4 tbsp soy sauce
- 1 tbsp tahini paste
- 1 tbsp cornflour
- 2 tsp sesame oil
- 2 tsp chilli oil
- 1 tbsp balsamic vinegar
- 1 tsp caster sugar
- 150ml (5fl oz) chicken stock, fresh or from powdered
- 2 tbsp sunflower oil
- 2 garlic cloves, finely chopped
- 2.5cm (1in) piece of fresh root ginger, finely chopped
- 350g (12oz) minced pork
- bunch of spring onions, finely chopped, to serve
- 50g (1¾oz) salted peanuts, roughly chopped, to serve (optional)

1 COOK THE NOODLES AND BROCCOLI

Cook the noodles in a large pan of boiling salted water according to the packet instructions. Drain well. Keep them in a bowl of cold water until needed (to stop them sticking together). Meanwhile, cook the broccoli for 2 minutes in a pan of boiling salted water, then drain and rinse under cold water. This stops the cooking process and preserves the colour of the broccoli, keeping it crisp and bright.

2 MAKE THE SAUCE

Whisk the soy sauce, tahini, and cornflour to a thick paste, then whisk in the sesame oil, chilli oil, balsamic vinegar, sugar, and stock.

3 STIR-FRY THE VEG

Heat the sunflower oil in a large wok and stir-fry the garlic and ginger for 1 minute, until it starts to colour. Add the pork and stir-fry over a high heat, breaking it up with a wooden spoon, until it browns. Add the sauce and allow to boil for about 2 minutes, until it thickens.

4 ADD THE NOODLES AND SERVE

Add the drained noodles and broccoli, stirring them well to make sure they are well coated with the sauce and heated through. Serve scattered with the spring onions and peanuts, if using.

PLAN OF ACTION!

 COOK NOODLES AND BROCCOLI → MAKE SAUCE →  STIR-FRY VEG → ADD NOODLES AND SERVE

STIR-FRY IN NO TIME

① GET SET...

- Grab a wok – the ideal pan for stir-frying. Being thin it heats up quickly, and its curved shape creates a large surface area for cooking.
- Avoid woks with non-stick coatings, which can prevent the wok reaching the high temperatures required for stir-frying.
- No wok? No worries – any large deep-sided frying pan will do!
- For stirring, use any heatproof spoon (the longer the handle the better, to keep your hand away from the heat). Be careful not to leave it in the wok unattended, as the heat may cause it to melt or burn.

② GET PREPPED...

- Prepare all your ingredients before you start – there won't be time later.
- Cut your ingredients into small, similar-sized pieces to allow quick and even cooking.
- Cook your rice or noodles first, then drain and set aside. Add to the wok once the other ingredients are ready.
- Use groundnut or sunflower oil for cooking (2 tbsp), as these oils can be heated to very high temperatures without burning.
- Heat the wok before adding the oil (oil will slow the heating process).
- Swirl the oil around the wok and wait until it is smoking hot before adding any ingredients.

③ GO!

- Add chillies and spices first so their flavours can infuse the cooking oil. Then add your ingredients according to how long each takes to cook:
  - Start with proteins, such as meat, fish, or tofu (150g/5½oz). Peanuts or boiled eggs can be added later.
  - Then add hard vegetables, such as carrot or broccoli (75g/2½oz).
  - Now add softer vegetables, such as onion, mushrooms, leafy greens, and peppers (75g/2½oz).
  - Add a pinch or splash (to taste) of seasonings, sauces, and herbs towards the end of cooking.
  - Finally, return the cooked rice or noodles to the wok to heat through (75g/2½oz, dried weight).

KEY STIR-FRY INGREDIENTS

PROTEINS

Beef • Pork • Chicken • Prawns • Calamari • Salmon • Peanuts • Tofu • Boiled eggs

VEGETABLES

Beansprouts • Onions • Spring onions • Shallots • Garlic • Bamboo shoots • Water chestnuts • Pak choi • Carrots • Green beans • Mangetout • Shiitake mushrooms • Enoki mushrooms • Edamame beans • Oyster mushrooms • Daikon radish • Cabbage • Napa cabbage • Soy bean sprouts

Stir-frying is the ultimate in quick cooking. Make sure your stir-fries are always spot on by following our three steps to success. Then, find out how to give your key stir-fry ingredients a cuisine-based makeover with a few traditional flavourings. The suggested quantities serve 1.

STIR-FRY FLAVOURS

KOREAN-STYLE

FLAVOURS Red pepper • Chilli powder • Red chilli paste • Korean soybean paste • Korean soy sauce • Sesame oil • Apricot syrup • Sake or mirin

TYPICAL INGREDIENTS Tofu • Napa cabbage • Soy bean sprouts • Daikon radish

VIETNAMESE-STYLE

FLAVOURS Cloves • Cassia bark • Star anise • Fish sauce • Lemongrass • Shrimp paste

TYPICAL INGREDIENTS Beef • Pork • Prawns • Calamari • Rice vermicelli • Flat rice noodles • Sticky rice • Oyster mushrooms • Pickled bamboo

JAPANESE-STYLE

FLAVOURS Shoyu or tamari • Mirin • Rice vinegar • Teriyaki sauce • Sake • Pickled ginger (gari)

TYPICAL INGREDIENTS Tofu • Eggs • Salmon • Shiitake mushrooms • Enoki mushrooms • Cabbage • Edamame beans • Daikon radish • Sticky rice • Soba noodles • Udon noodles • Mizuna (as a garnish)

INDONESIAN-STYLE

FLAVOURS Galangal • Shrimp paste • Palm sugar • Lime juice • Turmeric • Nutmeg • Kecap manis (a sweet, syrup-like soy sauce)

TYPICAL INGREDIENTS Eggs • Peanuts • Beef • Pork • Green beans • Spring onions • Mangetout • Shallots • Long-grain rice • Wheat noodles • Rice vermicelli • Flat rice noodles

THAI-STYLE

FLAVOURS Tamarind paste • Thai sweet basil • Lemongrass • Nam pla (fish sauce) • Thai shrimp paste • Lime juice

TYPICAL INGREDIENTS Prawns • Chicken • Peanuts • Eggs • Bean sprouts • Spring onions • Jasmine rice • Flat rice noodles • Rice vermicelli

SICHUAN-STYLE

FLAVOURS Sichuan peppercorns • Facing heaven pepper • Sesame paste • Ginger • Star anise • Cinnamon • Garlic

TYPICAL INGREDIENTS Peanuts • Egg noodles

RICE AND NOODLES

Sticky rice • Soba noodles • Udon noodles • Egg noodles • Short-grain white rice • Long-grain white rice • Jasmine rice • Flat rice noodles • Rice vermicelli • Wheat noodles

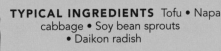

THAI-STYLE STIR-FRIED BEEF IN LETTUCE CUPS

This is a fun way to serve and eat stir-fry – in individual baby gem lettuce cups! You can tuck into this as it is, eating the lettuce cups with your hands, or serve with basmati rice or quinoa for a more substantial meal.

SERVES 4-6 • **READY IN** 15 mins

1 BLANCH THE BROCCOLI

Bring a large pan of water to the boil and add the broccoli, cooking it for just 1 minute before draining it and rinsing it under cold water to stop the cooking process. Set aside.

2 STIR-FRY THE FRESH INGREDIENTS

Heat the sunflower oil in a wok or a large, deep-sided frying pan. Add the spring onions, garlic, ginger, carrot, coriander stalks, and chilli, and fry for a couple of minutes until coloured slightly.

3 ADD THE BEEF

Add the minced beef and continue to fry over a high heat until the meat is well browned.

4 COMBINE, FLAVOUR, AND SERVE

Return the broccoli to the pan and add the fish sauce, soy sauce, lime juice, and sugar. Mix well, cooking for a minute or 2 until the broccoli is piping hot. Stir in the coriander leaves and divide between individual "cups" of baby gem lettuce.

Why not try substituting minced turkey, minced pork, tofu, or prawns for the beef?

1	2	3	4
BLANCH BROCCOLI	**STIR-FRY INGREDIENTS**	**ADD BEEF**	**COMBINE AND SERVE**

INGREDIENTS

100g (3½oz) broccoli florets, cut very small

2 tbsp sunflower oil

bunch of spring onions, finely chopped

2 garlic cloves, crushed

2.5cm (1in) fresh root ginger, finely chopped

1 large carrot, cut into strips

1 tbsp finely chopped coriander stalks, plus a handful of coriander leaves, roughly chopped

1 red chilli, deseeded and finely chopped

400g (14oz) minced beef

1 tbsp Thai fish sauce

2 tbsp soy sauce

1 tbsp lime juice

1 tsp caster sugar

baby gem lettuce leaves, to serve

INGREDIENTS

300g (10oz) medium or thick dried rice noodles

3 tbsp sunflower oil

2 eggs, lightly beaten

1 tsp shrimp paste (optional)

2 hot red chillies, deseeded and finely chopped

3 skinless boneless chicken breasts, cut into 5mm (¼in) slices

bunch of spring onions, finely chopped

splash of Thai fish sauce, such as nam pla

juice of 1 lime

1 tbsp demerara sugar

salt and freshly ground black pepper

150g (5½oz) unsalted peanuts, toasted in a dry wok or frying pan

handful of coriander leaves, finely chopped

lime wedges, to serve

5
COMBINE WITH
NOODLES

PAD THAI

Originating from road-side food stalls in Thailand, this zingy noodle dish is designed to be quick to cook and easy to assemble – ideal for the time-limited chef! Experiment with different kinds of rice noodles to find your favourite.

SERVES 4 • **READY IN** 20 mins

1 SOAK THE NOODLES

Put the noodles in a large bowl, cover with boiling water, and leave for 8 minutes, or until soft. Drain and set aside.

2 COOK THE EGG

Meanwhile, put 1 tbsp of the oil in a large wok over a high heat and swirl around the pan. Add the beaten egg and swirl it around the wok for about a minute, or until it begins to set – don't let it set completely – then remove, chop, and set aside.

3 STIR-FRY THE CHICKEN

Add the remaining 2 tbsp of oil to the pan, then add the shrimp paste, if using, and chillies, and stir. With the heat still high, add the chicken and stir vigorously for 5 minutes, or until it is no longer pink.

4 ADD FLAVOURINGS

Stir through the spring onions, fish sauce, lime juice, and sugar, and toss together well. Cook for a few minutes until the sugar has dissolved, then season well with salt and pepper. Return the egg to the pan.

5 COMBINE WITH THE NOODLES

Add the noodles to the pan and toss together to coat with the sauce, then add half the peanuts and half the coriander and toss again. Transfer to a large, shallow warmed serving bowl and scatter over the rest of the peanuts and coriander. Garnish with lime wedges to serve.

For a vegetarian option, omit the chicken, shrimp paste, and fish sauce and substitute fried tofu that's been marinated in soy sauce, crushed garlic, lime juice, and chilli.

OVEN-BAKED RISOTTO

This risotto needs much less of your time than the traditional method – instead of constantly stirring for 20 minutes, you fry everything briefly before popping it in the oven to do its thing!

SERVES 4 • **READY IN** 20–30 mins
SPECIAL EQUIPMENT Large, heavy-based flameproof casserole

INGREDIENTS

- 25g (scant 1oz) butter
- 1 tbsp olive oil
- 1 onion, finely chopped
- 2 garlic cloves, finely chopped
- 300g (10oz) mixed mushrooms, such as chestnut, shiitake, and oyster, roughly chopped
- 400g (14oz) risotto rice
- 800ml (1¼ pints) vegetable or chicken stock, fresh or from powdered
- 150ml (5fl oz) dry white wine
- salt and freshly ground black pepper
- 300g (10oz) cooked chicken, chopped into bite-sized pieces
- 40g (1¼oz) grated Grana Padano cheese, plus extra to serve
- 4 tbsp chopped parsley leaves

1 FRY THE ONION AND GARLIC

Preheat the oven to 200°C (400°F/Gas 6). Heat the butter and oil in a large, heavy-based flameproof casserole over a low heat. Once the butter has melted, add the onion and garlic, and cook gently for 3–4 minutes.

2 ADD THE MUSHROOMS, RICE, AND STOCK

Add the mushrooms and rice and stir well to coat in the butter and oil. Pour in the stock and wine, bring to the boil, season, and stir well.

3 COVER AND BAKE

Cover and cook in the oven for about 15 minutes, or until the rice is tender, stirring a couple of times.

4 ADD THE CHICKEN AND CHEESE

Remove from the oven and stir in the chicken, Grana Padano cheese, and parsley. Return to the oven for 2–3 minutes, or until the chicken is heated through. Serve with pepper and extra Grana Padano, for sprinkling.

For a spinach and hot-smoked salmon risotto, omit the mushrooms and chicken, and stir in 300g (10oz) flaked, hot-smoked salmon fillets and 100g (3½oz) spinach 5 minutes before the end of the cooking time.

PLAN OF ACTION!

1 **FRY ONION AND GARLIC** → 2 **ADD MUSHROOMS, RICE, AND STOCK** → 3 **COVER AND BAKE** → 4 **ADD CHICKEN AND CHEESE**

ARANCINI

A fantastic way to use up leftover rice and risotto, these Italian stuffed rice balls make a light and tasty supper. Serve alongside a crisp green salad and, if you wish, a spicy fresh tomato sauce.

MAKES 12 • **READY IN** 20 mins, plus resting

INGREDIENTS

- 400g (14oz) cooked, cold risotto
- 60g (2oz) mozzarella cheese, cut into 12 x 1cm (½in) cubes
- 4 tbsp plain flour
- 1 egg, beaten
- 50g (1¾oz) day-old breadcrumbs or Japanese panko breadcrumbs
- 1 litre (1¾ pints) sunflower oil, for deep-frying

1 MOULD THE RISOTTO BALLS

Keep your hands damp to mould the risotto balls. Take a walnut-sized spoonful of the risotto rice and mould it, in your palm, so it creates a flattened circle. Place a cube of the mozzarella in the middle of the rice and mould the rice around it, rolling it to make a ball. Be careful that the mozzarella is well covered, and take care to pack the risotto tightly around. Continue until you have 12 balls.

2 ROLL IN BREADCRUMBS

Put the flour, egg, and breadcrumbs separately in 3 wide, shallow bowls. Roll each risotto ball first in the flour, then in the egg, and finally coat it well in the breadcrumbs. Place on a plate, cover with cling film, and rest in the fridge for at least 30 minutes (this will help the coating to stick).

3 HEAT THE OIL

Heat the oil in a large, heavy-based saucepan to a depth of 10cm (4in). It will be ready to use when a small piece of bread dropped in sizzles and turns golden brown.

4 FRY THE ARANCINI

Fry the risotto balls a few at a time, for 2 minutes, until golden brown all over. Remove with a slotted spoon and drain on kitchen paper. Keep warm in the oven while you cook the rest.

TIP - You can make arancini with all sorts of risottos, and any leftover cooked rice, but ensure that the kind you use is fairly smooth in texture, as then the mixture will adhere more easily to the breadcrumb coating. If you're making these with leftover Oven-Baked Risotto (see opposite), ensure that the mushrooms are chopped up into small pieces.

PLAN OF ACTION!

1 MOULD RISOTTO BALLS → 2 ROLL IN BREADCRUMBS → 3 HEAT OIL → 4 FRY ARANCINI

SIMPLE STUFFED VEGETABLES

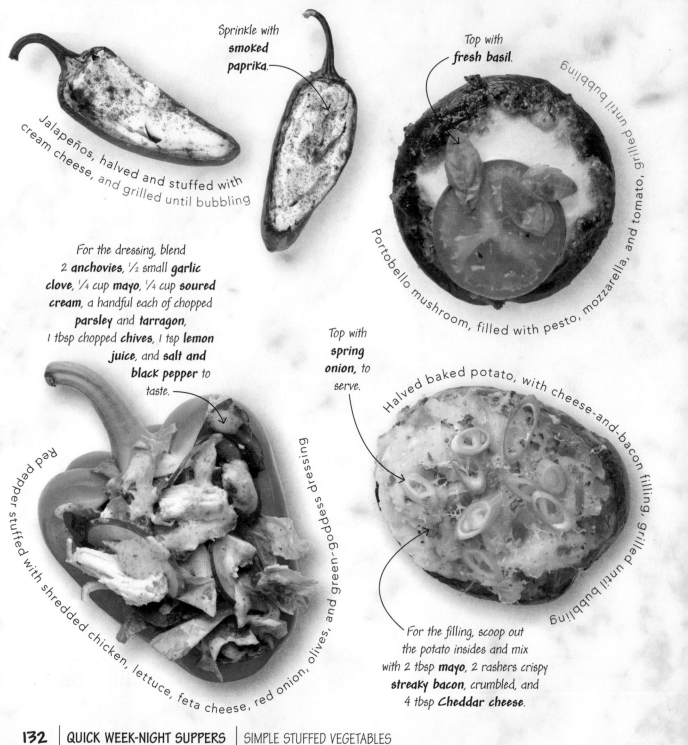

Jalapeños, halved and stuffed with cream cheese, and grilled until bubbling

Sprinkle with **smoked paprika**.

Top with **fresh basil**.

Portobello mushroom, filled with pesto, mozzarella, and tomato, grilled until bubbling

For the dressing, blend 2 **anchovies**, ½ small **garlic clove**, ¼ cup **mayo**, ¼ cup **soured cream**, a handful each of chopped **parsley** and **tarragon**, 1 tbsp chopped **chives**, 1 tsp **lemon juice**, and **salt and black pepper** to taste.

Top with **spring onion**, to serve.

Red pepper stuffed with shredded chicken, lettuce, feta cheese, red onion, olives, and green-goddess dressing

Halved baked potato, with cheese-and-bacon filling, grilled until bubbling

For the filling, scoop out the potato insides and mix with 2 tbsp **mayo**, 2 rashers crispy **streaky bacon**, crumbled, and 4 tbsp **Cheddar cheese**.

These delightful stuffed vegetables are as delicious as they are eye-catching. They're easy to prepare for comforting, everyday dinners and look great for when you're entertaining friends. Instead of these fillings, you could use mashed sweet potato or corn, seasoned breadcrumbs, rice, or quinoa.

Halved and slightly hollowed out avocado with an egg cracked in, topped with cayenne pepper and sea salt

Bake at 220°C (425°F/Gas 7) until the egg is set.

Drizzle with **olive oil** and grill until bubbling.

Tomato stuffed with cooked couscous, fresh basil and oregano, and topped with Parmesan

Halved aubergine stuffed with roughly chopped chorizo, onion, and red and green peppers

Top with **ricotta cheese** and bake at 180°C (350°F/Gas 4) until golden.

ONE-POT MEALS

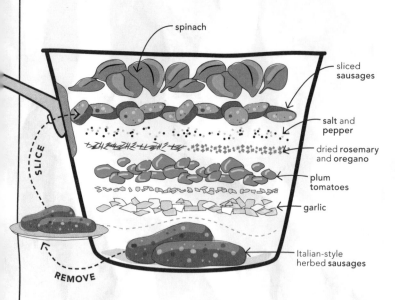

spinach

sliced sausages

salt and pepper

dried rosemary and oregano

plum tomatoes

garlic

SLICE

REMOVE

Italian-style herbed sausages

MEDITERRANEAN MIX

1. Heat 1 tbsp **olive oil** over a medium heat.

2. Add 200g (7oz) good quality Italian-style herbed **sausages** and cook for 3 minutes on each side, or until browned and cooked through. Remove the sausages and set aside.

3. Stir in 1 chopped onion, 2 finely chopped **garlic** cloves, and 400g (14oz) chopped fresh **plum tomatoes**, along with 1 tbsp dried **oregano**, 1 tbsp dried **rosemary**, **salt**, and **pepper**. Cook for 5 minutes.

4. Return the sausages, sliced, to the pan, and add 2 big handfuls of fresh **spinach**. Stir together to wilt the spinach. Serve with **crusty bread**.

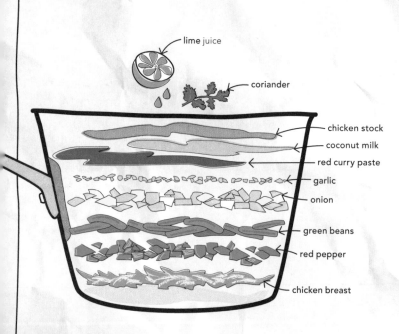

lime juice

coriander

chicken stock

coconut milk

red curry paste

garlic

onion

green beans

red pepper

chicken breast

RED CURRY IN A HURRY

1. Heat 1 tbsp **coconut oil** over a medium heat.

2. Add 1 **chicken breast**, cut into strips, and fry until the meat is cooked through.

3. Place 400g (14oz) chopped **red peppers**, 300g (10oz) sliced **green beans**, 1 chopped **onion**, and 2 finely sliced cloves of **garlic** into the pan. Stir to coat.

4. Stir in 2 tbsp **red curry paste**, 300ml (10fl oz) **coconut milk**, and 60ml (2fl oz) **chicken stock**. Bring to a rapid simmer, and cook for 10–12 minutes, stirring frequently.

5. Add a squeeze of fresh **lime** juice, garnish with **coriander**, and serve with pre-cooked **basmati rice**.

What could be simpler and quicker than cooking a whole meal in just one pot or pan? With these recipes you can have a satisfying supper for two on the table in 20 minutes, and only one pot to wash up! All you need is a large skillet or deep-sided frying pan and a few simple ingredients.

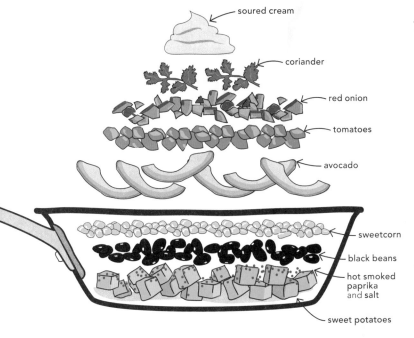

VEG-MEX MEDLEY

1 Melt 1 tbsp **coconut oil** over a medium heat.

2 Add 500g (1lb 2oz) diced **sweet potatoes**, 1 tsp **hot smoked paprika**, and a pinch of **salt**. Cook for 10 minutes, stirring occasionally.

3 Add 100g (3½oz) canned **black beans**, drained, and 100g (3½oz) canned **sweetcorn**, drained. Cook for a further 5 minutes.

4 Remove from the heat and top with 1 sliced **avocado**, 200g (7oz) diced **tomatoes**, 1 diced **red onion**, and 100g (3½oz) **coriander**.

5 Garnish with soured cream.

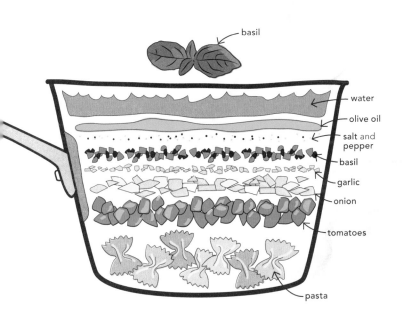

ONE-POT PASTA

1 Add 350g (12oz) **pasta**, such as farfalle, 200g (7oz) chopped fresh **tomatoes**, 1 chopped **onion**, 4 finely chopped **garlic** cloves, a large handful of torn **basil**, **salt**, **pepper**, 4 tbsp **olive oil**, and 1 litre (1¾ pints) **water**.

2 Bring to the boil over a high heat and simmer,

3 Garnish with fresh basil and serve.

PESTO, PRONTO!

This versatile Italian sauce can be tossed with cooked pasta, spread on crostini, beaten with crème fraîche for a dip, or even used on tarts or pizza bases. Blend the ingredients in a food processor or pestle and mortar, then adjust to taste. Each recipe makes 1 jar (300g/10oz), which will keep in the fridge for up to 1 week.

CLASSIC BASIL
The ultimate green pesto, bursting with fresh, herby flavours.

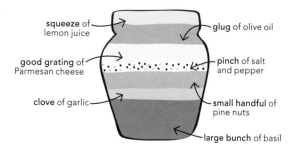

squeeze of lemon juice
glug of olive oil
good grating of Parmesan cheese
pinch of salt and pepper
clove of garlic
small handful of pine nuts
large bunch of basil

SUN-DRIED TOMATO
Perfect on pizza or in a sandwich, this red pesto has great depth of flavour.

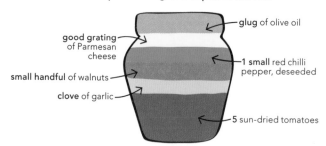

glug of olive oil
good grating of Parmesan cheese
small handful of walnuts
clove of garlic
1 small red chilli pepper, deseeded
5 sun-dried tomatoes

ROCKET
A popular variation, rocket pesto works well with fish and chicken.

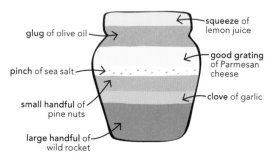

glug of olive oil
squeeze of lemon juice
pinch of sea salt
good grating of Parmesan cheese
small handful of pine nuts
clove of garlic
large handful of wild rocket

AUBERGINE
The char-grilled aubergine is like a burst of sunshine in this tasty pesto.

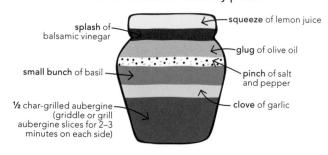

splash of balsamic vinegar
squeeze of lemon juice
glug of olive oil
small bunch of basil
pinch of salt and pepper
clove of garlic
½ char-grilled aubergine (griddle or grill aubergine slices for 2–3 minutes on each side)

ROASTED RED PEPPER
Sweet and tangy, try this red pesto with cheese and crackers.

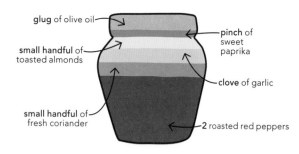

glug of olive oil
pinch of sweet paprika
small handful of toasted almonds
clove of garlic
small handful of fresh coriander
2 roasted red peppers

MINT
This fresh-tasting pesto marries mint with creamy, salty feta.

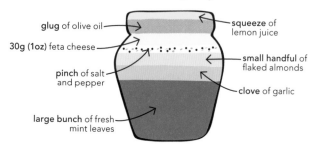

glug of olive oil
squeeze of lemon juice
30g (1oz) feta cheese
small handful of flaked almonds
pinch of salt and pepper
clove of garlic
large bunch of fresh mint leaves

BROCCOLI AND BLUE CHEESE PASTA SAUCE

Stir this delicious sauce through any pasta shape for a simple and quick dinner. For four people, cook about 400g (14oz) of dried pasta according to the packet instructions.

SERVES 4 • **READY IN** 20 mins

SPECIAL EQUIPMENT Food processor

INGREDIENTS

- 250g (9oz) broccoli, cut into bite-sized florets
- 200ml (7fl oz) half-fat crème fraîche
- 200g (7oz) Dolcelatte or Gorgonzola cheese, rind removed and roughly chopped
- finely grated zest of 1 lemon, plus 1 tbsp lemon juice
- ¼ tsp ground nutmeg
- freshly ground black pepper
- 3 tbsp chopped walnuts, to serve

❶ PREPARE THE BROCCOLI PURÉE

Place the broccoli in a steamer and steam for about 5 minutes, or until just tender. Drain well and transfer to a food processor. Whizz to a smooth purée.

❷ MAKE THE SAUCE

While the broccoli is steaming, make the sauce. Place the crème fraîche and cheese in a saucepan. Cook over a low heat, stirring constantly, until well combined and smooth. Then stir in the lemon zest, lemon juice, and nutmeg. Season with a good grinding of pepper and stir well.

❸ COMBINE AND SERVE

Add the broccoli purée to the cheese mixture and stir well to combine. To serve, pour the sauce over cooked pasta, mix to coat, and sprinkle with the walnuts.

> For a **milder** sauce, try replacing the blue cheese with cream cheese and a handful of grated Parmesan.

 **PLAN OF ACTION!**   **❶ PREPARE BROCCOLI** → **❷ MAKE SAUCE** → **❸ COMBINE AND SERVE**

PRAWN AND GARLIC "COURGETTI"

Also known as "zoodles" (zucchini noodles) the spaghetti-like ribbons of courgette in this quick and enticing dish offer a healthy, carb- and gluten-free alternative to pasta.

SERVES 4 • **READY IN** 20 mins
SPECIAL EQUIPMENT Julienne peeler

INGREDIENTS

- 6 courgettes
- salt and freshly ground black pepper
- 12 raw prawns, shelled and deveined
- 1 tbsp olive oil, plus 1 extra
- 1 garlic clove, crushed
- squeeze of lemon juice lemon

① MAKE THE COURGETTI
Cut off a thin slice along the length of each courgette (this stops them rolling around) and place on a chopping board. Use a julienne peeler to slice the courgettes into thin ribbons, stopping and rotating each courgette when you reach the seeds.

② SAUTÉ THE PRAWNS
Heat the oil in a large frying pan. Add the garlic and prawns and sauté until the prawns are pink and cooked through. Remove from the heat.

③ BLANCH THE COURGETTI
While the prawns are cooking, blanch (briefly boil) the courgetti. Place enough water to cover the courgetti in a large saucepan. Add a pinch of salt and bring to the boil. Then add the courgetti, cook for 1 minute, and remove. Plunge the courgetti into a bowl of ice water to stop the cooking process. Drain well.

④ COMBINE AND SERVE
Drain the courgetti and place on a serving dish. Drizzle over 1 tablespoon of oil, season to taste, and add a squeeze of lemon juice. Toss to mix, top with the shrimp, and serve.

For a **vegetarian** option, omit the prawns, stir through some pesto sauce (see p136), and top with halved cherry tomatoes.

PLAN OF ACTION!
 ❶ MAKE COURGETTI → ❷ SAUTÉ PRAWNS → ❸ BLANCH COURGETTI → ❹ COMBINE AND SERVE

PEA AND PANCETTA PASTA

This meal can be on the table in just 15 minutes! It's a speedy pasta dish that relies on a few store-cupboard essentials to make a satisfying supper. If you use shell pasta, such as conchigliette, the peas and pieces of pancetta nestle neatly inside.

SERVES 4 • **READY IN** 15 mins

- -

1 COOK THE PASTA AND PEAS

Cook the pasta in boiling salted water according to the packet instructions. A minute or two before the end of cooking, throw the peas in with the pasta to cook through. Drain (reserving a ladleful of the cooking water) and return it to the pan with the reserved water.

2 FRY THE PANCETTA

Meanwhile, heat the oil in a large frying pan. Cook the pancetta for 3–5 minutes over a medium heat until crispy. Add the butter and garlic and cook for a further minute, then remove from the heat.

3 TOSS TOGETHER AND SEASON

Toss the garlicky pancetta through the pasta and peas, and follow with the Parmesan cheese. Season well and serve with the extra Parmesan cheese.

TIP – There's no need to peel the garlic, just pop a clove into the crusher with its skin on.

You can use chopped up bacon rashers if you don't have any pancetta. Choose streaky and smoked bacon, as it is most like pancetta in flavour.

PLAN OF ACTION!

1 COOK PASTA → 2 FRY PANCETTA → 3 TOSS TOGETHER

INGREDIENTS

300g (10oz) dried shell pasta, such as conchigliette

salt and freshly ground black pepper

150g (5½oz) frozen peas or petits pois

2 tbsp olive oil

200g (7oz) pancetta lardons

2 tbsp butter

2 garlic cloves, crushed

50g (1¾oz) finely grated Parmesan, plus extra to serve

CHICKEN FAJITAS

These Mexican-style wraps are quick to prepare and fun to assemble. They are traditionally made with chicken or beef, but see pages 144–7 for lots more ideas for fillings.

SERVES 4 • READY IN 20 mins

FOR THE FAJITAS
- 2 large skinless boneless chicken breasts, sliced
- 1 red onion, deseeded and cut into 1cm (½in) slices
- 1 red pepper, deseeded and cut into 1cm (½in) slices
- 2 tbsp sunflower oil
- 8 tortillas

FOR THE MARINADE
- 2 tbsp olive oil
- juice of 1 lime
- 2 tsp ground cumin

- 1 tsp smoked paprika
- 1 tsp dried oregano
- 1 tsp cayenne pepper or chilli powder
- salt and freshly ground black pepper

FOR THE SALSA
- 4 large ripe tomatoes
- 1 green chilli
- ½ red onion
- handful of coriander
- juice of 1 lime
- glug of olive oil

MAKE THE CHICKEN MIX

1 SLICE

chicken breasts

2 SLICE

red onion

red pepper

3 MIX THEN MARINATE

olive oil

lime

cumin

smoked paprika

oregano

cayenne pepper or chilli powder

salt

pepper

Combine the sliced chicken, onion, and red pepper with the marinade ingredients.

Chop your fajita ingredients into pieces of the same size for even cooking.

WHILE THE MIX IS MARINATING, MAKE THE SALSA.

MAKE THE SALSA

4 CHOP

tomatoes

red onion

green chilli

coriander

Chop the salsa ingredients into same-sized pieces.

5 MIX

olive oil

lime

pepper

Combine all the salsa ingredients.

FRY THE CHICKEN MIX AND WARM THE TORTILLA

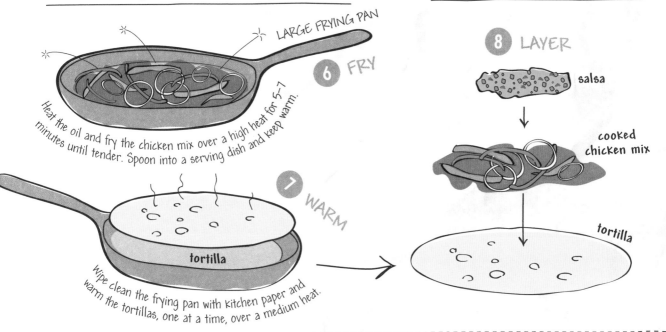

LARGE FRYING PAN

6 FRY

Heat the oil and fry the chicken mix over a high heat for 5–7 minutes until tender. Spoon into a serving dish and keep warm.

7 WARM

tortilla

Wipe clean the frying pan with kitchen paper and warm the tortillas, one at a time, over a medium heat.

BUILD THE FAJITA

8 LAYER

salsa

cooked chicken mix

tortilla

FOLDING YOUR FAJITA

1. Place the filling on the tortilla, leaving the bottom quarter empty.

2. Fold up the tortilla from the bottom edge.

3. Fold one side over...

4. ... then fold the other side over.

FAJITA FILLINGS

Tuna mayo with sweetcorn and salad leaves

Warm the **sardines** over a low heat.

Canned sardines in tomato sauce with mixed salad leaves

Smoked salmon, cream cheese, and griddled courgette

Drizzle of **balsamic** vinegar.

Grated Cheddar cheese, cherry tomatoes, cucumber, and mayo

Fajitas, or Mexican-style wraps, are such a versatile choice. It's so easy to replace traditional chicken fillings (see pp142–43) with appetizing meat, fish, or veggie alternatives – either cooked fresh or using up leftovers. Here are some fab fillings to try.

Cream cheese, roasted sweet potato, raw spinach leaves, and chilli flakes

Leftover chilli con carne with rocket leaves, soured cream, and paprika

Cooked prawns and thousand island dressing with salad

Drizzle with extra virgin **olive oil**.

Hummus and roasted carrots with sunflower seeds and rocket leaves

SPEEDY SALSAS

Why not transform your meal into a Mexican-style feast by adding one of these sensational salsas to your plate? They're also great for serving with tortilla chips or nachos when you've got friends over. Simply dice each ingredient into small, same-size pieces, mix it all up, then adjust to taste and eat as soon as possible!

PICO DE GALLO
This quick and easy salsa goes well with grilled steak or prawns.

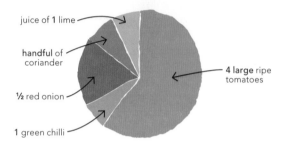

juice of 1 lime

handful of coriander

½ red onion

1 green chilli

4 large ripe tomatoes

GUACAMOLE
The traditional accompaniment for tacos and fajitas.

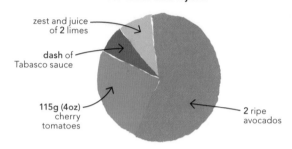

zest and juice of 2 limes

dash of Tabasco sauce

115g (4oz) cherry tomatoes

2 ripe avocados

MANGO SALSA
A sweet salsa that's great with jerk chicken or spice-rubbed salmon.

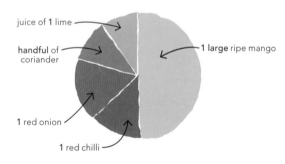

juice of 1 lime

handful of coriander

1 red onion

1 red chilli

1 large ripe mango

SWEETCORN SALSA
A delicious spicy salsa that's great with barbecued food.

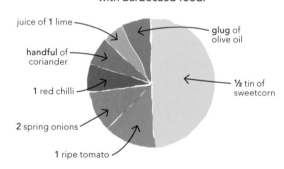

juice of 1 lime

handful of coriander

1 red chilli

2 spring onions

1 ripe tomato

glug of olive oil

½ tin of sweetcorn

PEACH SALSA
This fresh, fruity salsa is fantastic with grilled chicken or fish.

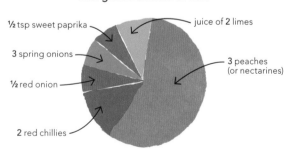

½ tsp sweet paprika

3 spring onions

½ red onion

2 red chillies

juice of 2 limes

3 peaches (or nectarines)

SALSA CRIOLLA
This tangy salsa is often served as an accompaniment to seafood.

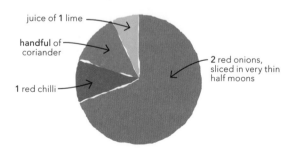

juice of 1 lime

handful of coriander

1 red chilli

2 red onions, sliced in very thin half moons

BLACK-EYED BEAN, SPINACH, AND TOMATO CURRY

A delicious and nutritious meal, this curry makes for a satisfying week-night supper that's quicker and cheaper than ordering a takeaway. Yogurt adds creaminess to the sauce – just be careful not to overcook it, as it will separate.

SERVES 4 • **READY IN** 20 mins

- -

❶ SOFTEN THE ONION

Heat the oil in a large saucepan and add the mustard seeds. When they start to pop, add the garlic, curry leaves, and onion. Cook over a medium heat for 5 minutes, or until the onion is soft.

❷ COOK THE TOMATO AND SPINACH

Add the green chillies, chilli powder, coriander, and turmeric. Mix well and add the tomato pieces. Stir, then add the spinach. Cook over a low heat for 5 minutes.

❸ ADD THE BEANS AND SERVE

Finally, add the black-eyed beans and salt to taste. Cook for another minute, or until everything is hot. Remove the pan from the heat and slowly add the yogurt, stirring well. Serve warm with naan breads or rice.

TIP – When yogurt is heated too much it separates into solid and liquid layers (curds and whey). Adding the yogurt gradually as the dish cools will ensure that it retains its creaminess.

PLAN OF ACTION!

1. SOFTEN ONION → 2. COOK TOMATO AND SPINACH → 3. ADD BEANS

INGREDIENTS

3 tbsp sunflower oil

½ tsp mustard seeds

2 garlic cloves, finely chopped

10 curry leaves

1 large onion, chopped

2 green chillies, slit lengthways and deseeded

½ tsp chilli powder

1 tsp ground coriander

½ tsp ground turmeric

3 tomatoes, chopped

100g (3½oz) spinach, chopped

400g can black-eyed beans, rinsed and drained

salt

300g (10oz) plain yogurt

naan breads or rice, to serve

HEART OF PALM AND CRAYFISH GREEN CURRY

Hearts of palm – the edible centres of young palm shoots – have a crunch that offers a textural contrast to the creamy spicy sauce. For added colour, why not throw in some cherry tomatoes at step 2?

SERVES 4 • **READY IN** 20 mins

INGREDIENTS

- 5 tbsp coconut cream
- 4 tbsp Thai green curry paste
- 400g can hearts of palm, drained and cut into bite-sized pieces
- 4–5 baby sweetcorn, each cut in half lengthways
- light soy sauce, to taste
- 400ml can coconut milk
- 150g (5½oz) cooked crayfish tails
- a few pea aubergines (optional)
- 3 kaffir lime leaves, torn
- 3 green chillies, deseeded and thinly sliced at an angle
- handful of Thai (or ordinary) basil leaves, torn
- jasmine rice, to serve

❶ HEAT THE PASTE, HEARTS OF PALM, AND CORN

Heat the coconut cream in a saucepan, add the curry paste, and cook over a high heat for 3 minutes, stirring regularly. Add the hearts of palm and corn, and fry for a further 3 minutes or until the paste looks scrambled and smells cooked. Season with soy sauce.

❷ SIMMER THE REMAINING INGREDIENTS AND SERVE

Pour in the coconut milk, stirring gently. Bring to a boil and add the remaining ingredients except the basil. Check the seasoning and adjust if necessary. Simmer for 2 minutes, then stir in the basil. Spoon over jasmine rice in bowls and serve.

If you can't find heart of palm, try green pepper, asparagus, or cooked new potatoes instead.

PLAN OF ACTION!

❶ HEAT PASTE, HEARTS OF PALM, AND CORN ⟶ ❷ SIMMER AND SERVE

BEEF STROGANOFF

This classic Russian dish with a rich creamy sauce is a quick alternative to a stew. It works particularly well with pasta, but you could pair it with rice or mashed potatoes instead.

SERVES 4 • **READY IN** 20 mins

INGREDIENTS

- 4 tbsp olive oil
- 400g (14oz) steak, such as rump, very thinly sliced
- 1 onion, finely chopped
- 150g (5½oz) button mushrooms, sliced
- 1 tbsp butter
- 2 tbsp plain flour
- 300ml (10fl oz) beef stock
- 4 heaped tbsp crème fraîche or soured cream
- 1 heaped tsp paprika
- salt and freshly ground black pepper
- ½ tbsp lemon juice
- 1 tbsp chopped dill (optional)
- buttered tagliatelle, to serve

1 SEAR THE STEAK AND SET ASIDE

Heat 2 tbsp of the oil in a large, deep-sided frying pan. Sear the steak in batches over a high heat, cooking until it just colours. Set aside.

2 FRY THE ONION AND MUSHROOMS

Heat the remaining 2 tbsp of oil in the pan and fry the onion and mushrooms over a medium heat for 5 minutes until the mushrooms are golden brown, taking care not to burn the onions.

3 ADD THE STOCK AND THICKEN THE SAUCE

Add the butter and sprinkle the flour over, stirring it in. Gradually stir in the stock and cook for a few minutes until the sauce thickens. Stir in the crème fraîche and paprika and season to taste.

4 RETURN THE BEEF AND SERVE

Return the beef and heat it through. Add the lemon with the dill (if using). Serve over buttered tagliatelle.

PLAN OF ACTION!
1 SEAR STEAK → 2 FRY ONION AND MUSHROOMS → 3 ADD STOCK AND THICKEN SAUCE → 4 RETURN BEEF AND SERVE

MARGHERITA IN MINUTES

This homemade margherita can be ready in less time than it takes for a takeaway to arrive, and will taste much better! Add extra toppings if you fancy.

MAKES 4 • **READY IN** 20 mins, plus rising (optional)

- 500g (1lb 2oz) "00" or strong white flour, plus extra for dusting
- 7g sachet of fast-action dried yeast
- pinch of salt
- 4 tbsp olive oil, plus extra for greasing

FOR THE TOPPING
- 2–3 tbsp tomato purée or passata
- 150g (5½oz) mozzarella, sliced into thin rounds
- handful of fresh basil leaves, torn

MAKE THE DOUGH

1 SIFT

SIEVE

flour

salt

dried yeast

Sift the flour into a large bowl and add the dried yeast and salt.

2 MIX

warm water

olive oil

Make a well in the mixture.

Slowly add 350ml (12fl oz) warm water. Mix, adding in the olive oil gradually, until it forms a soft dough.

KNEAD THE DOUGH

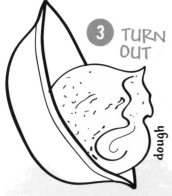

3 TURN OUT

dough

dusting of flour

4 KNEAD

Firmly knead and fold the dough until it becomes soft and spongy.

5 LEAVE TO RISE

TEA TOWEL

Place in an oiled bowl and cover.

Leave the dough in a warm place for 30–40 minutes.

ROLL IT OUT

6 ROLL

dusting of flour

Preheat the oven to 240°C (475°F/Gas 9). Roll out ¼ of the dough into a thin round, about 20cm (8in) wide, and transfer to a baking sheet.

> **If time** is short, you don't have to wait for the dough to rise – just make sure you roll it very thinly before baking.

ADD TOPPINGS AND BAKE

mozzarella

black pepper

Spread passata over the base with a spoon.

7 TOP AND BAKE

Add the toppings (except the basil) and bake in the oven for 10 minutes. Serve topped with the fresh basil leaves.

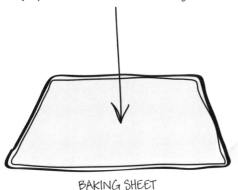

BAKING SHEET

PIZZA TOPPER

START

❶ BASE

TRADITIONAL – see pages 152–3 for the recipe.

FLATBREAD – use a pre-made tortilla, naan, pita, or other flatbread.

❷ SAUCE

TOMATO – combine 4 tbsp tomato purée, 1 crushed garlic clove, and a glug of extra virgin olive oil.

CHILLI-TOMATO – add 1 tsp dried chilli flakes to the recipe above.

BBQ SAUCE – see page 68 for the recipe.

BIANCO – melt 2 tbsp butter in a medium pan and stir in 3 tbsp flour. Cook over a medium heat, stirring constantly, for 3–4 minutes. Slowly whisk in 240ml (8fl oz) milk. Simmer for 5 minutes, or until thickened, then stir in a large handful of grated Parmesan cheese.

PESTO – see pages 136–7 for recipes.

❸ CHEESE

MOZZARELLA – 1 ball or 125g (4½oz) mozzarella pearls, torn.

CHEDDAR – 300g (10oz), grated.

FETA – 200g (7oz), crumbled.

GOAT'S CHEESE – 200g (7oz), sliced into rounds.

BLUE CHEESE – 150g (5½oz), crumbled.

❺ VEG

MARINATED ARTICHOKE HEARTS – 50g (1¾oz), drained.

OLIVES – 50g (1¾oz), sliced.

PICKLED JALAPEÑO – 50g (1¾oz), sliced.

ROASTED GARLIC – 5 cloves.

CARAMELIZED ONIONS – 200g (7oz).

RED ONION or **SHALLOTS** – 100g (3½oz), thinly sliced.

MUSHROOMS – 100g (3½oz), sliced.

PEPPERS or **ROASTED PEPPERS** – 100g (3½oz), thinly sliced.

AUBERGINE – 75g (2½oz), sliced and grilled.

COURGETTE – 100g (3½oz), finely sliced.

ASPARAGUS – 75g (2½oz), shaved into fine slices using a vegetable peeler.

SWEETCORN – ½ small can, drained.

AND/OR

❹ FRUIT

CHERRY TOMATOES – 100g (3½oz), halved.

SUN-DRIED TOMATOES – 50g (1¾oz), chopped or quartered.

APPLES or **PEARS** – 150g (5½oz), thinly sliced.

PEACHES – 100g (3½oz), sliced.

FRESH FIGS – 200g (7oz), sliced.

PINEAPPLE CHUNKS – 100g (3½oz).

GRAPES – 100g (3½oz), halved.

Once you've mastered the margherita (see pp152–3), it's time to put your speedy pizza skills to the test with our pizza topper flowchart! Simply follow the steps below to mix and match your favourite ingredients. Try not to overload your pizza with toppings, though, as the base will take longer to cook through.

AND/OR

6 PROTEIN

PEPPERONI – 200g (7oz).
PARMA HAM – 150g (5½oz).
HAM – 150g (5½oz).
SALSICCIA SAUSAGE – 250g (9oz).
CHORIZO – 150g (5½oz).
PANCETTA – 100g (3½oz).
CHICKEN BREAST – 150g (5½oz), grilled and shredded.
PRAWNS – 200g (7oz).
TUNA – ½ can, flaked.
ANCHOVIES – 6–8, drained.
EGGS – 4, cracked on top 6–8 minutes before the end of cooking.
WALNUTS – 1 handful, crushed.
PINE NUTS – 1 handful.

7 SEASONINGS

DRIED HERBS, such as oregano, basil, rosemary, or thyme – 2 tbsp, sprinkled over.
GARLIC POWDER – 1 tsp, sprinkled over.
PAPRIKA – 1 tsp, sprinkled over.
SMOKED PAPRIKA – ½ tsp, sprinkled over.
DRIED CHILLI FLAKES – ½ tsp, sprinkled over.
BLACK PEPPER – freshly ground.

8 OILS

OLIVE OIL, **MELTED BUTTER**, or **MELTED COCONUT OIL** – 1 tbsp brushed onto the crust and drizzled over the pizza before baking.
TRUFFLE OIL, **CHILLI OIL**, or **GARLIC OIL** – 1 tsp drizzled over the baked pizza before serving.

DIPS AND SAUCES

SOURED CREAM • GARLIC MAYO • SMOKY AÏOLI • BLUE CHEESE SAUCE • BALSAMIC GLAZE • TAPENADE • SWEET CHILLI SAUCE

(See also pages 166–7 and 200–1.)

FINISH

9 GARNISHES

PARMESAN – 50g (1¾oz), grated or shaved over the baked pizza before serving.
FRESH BASIL – 1 handful, torn.
RICOTTA CHEESE – 100g (3½oz), spooned over.
AVOCADO – 1, sliced.

INGREDIENTS

1 tsp smoked paprika

1 tsp cayenne pepper

1 tsp garlic powder

½ tsp dried thyme

1 tsp soft light brown sugar

½ tsp salt

4 skinless salmon fillets, approx.150g (5½oz) each

2 tbsp olive oil

PLAN OF ACTION!

1 GRIND SPICES → 2 PREPARE SALMON → 3 GRILL SALMON

CAJUN-SPICED SALMON

This simple, Louisiana-inspired rub instantly livens up any fish, and it's particularly good with salmon. You can serve the salmon with a thinly sliced onion, avocado, and cherry tomato salad for a light, flavoursome supper.

SERVES 4 • **READY IN 15 mins**

① GRIND THE SPICES
Combine the spices, thyme, sugar, and salt in a mortar and pestle or a spice grinder. Grind to a fine powder.

② PREPARE THE SALMON
Rub the mixture over both sides of the fish, cover with cling film, and leave to rest in the fridge while you prepare the grill.

③ GRILL THE SALMON
Preheat the grill on its highest setting and line a grill pan with foil. Brush the fish with a little oil on both sides, being careful not to dislodge the spice rub, and grill for 3–4 minutes on each side, depending on its thickness.

TIP – The salmon can be marinated in the rub and frozen, uncooked. Defrost thoroughly before cooking from the start of step 3. You can also double the quantity of spice rub and seal the remainder in an airtight jar for future use.

This spice rub is great for seasoning chicken, potato, or sweet potato wedges as well as fish.

THE PERFECT STEAK

Good-quality steak needs very little embellishment. Simply pan-frying it in butter with a little salt and pepper will give you perfect results in an instant.

SERVES 2 • READY IN 6–14 mins, plus resting

- 2 x 3cm (1¼in) thick beef sirloin or rib-eye steaks
- 1–2 tbsp butter, softened
- salt and freshly ground black pepper

> **For rare,** cook for 6–8 minutes in total.
> **For medium,** cook for 10–12 minutes in total.
> **For well done,** cook for 12–14 minutes in total.
> (The thickness of the steak will affect the cooking time.)

COOK THE STEAK

1 ADD

HEAVY-BASED FRYING PAN

TONGS

butter

steak

Heat the butter over a high heat until it simmers, then add the steak.

2 SEAR

SLOTTED SPATULA

Press down the steak with a slotted spatula, reduce the heat slightly, and sear for 1–2 minutes.

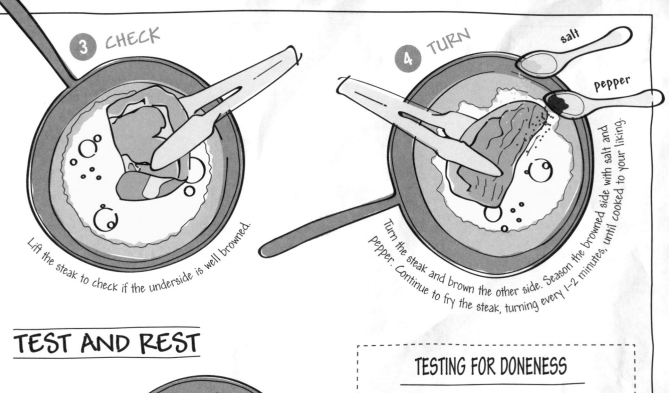

3 CHECK

Lift the steak to check if the underside is well browned.

4 TURN

salt

pepper

Turn the steak and brown the other side. Season the browned side with salt and pepper. Continue to fry the steak, turning every 1–2 minutes, until cooked to your liking.

TEST AND REST

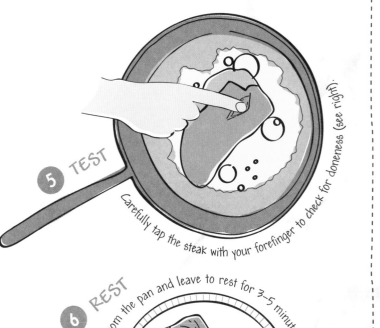

5 TEST

Carefully tap the steak with your forefinger to check for doneness (see right).

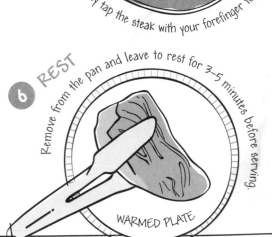

6 REST

Remove from the pan and leave to rest for 3–5 minutes before serving.

WARMED PLATE

TESTING FOR DONENESS

1. Rare Hold your hand with the fingers extended gently forwards. Prod the muscle between thumb and forefinger. This is how a rare steak should feel.

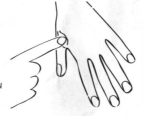

2. Medium Stretch out your fingers as far as they will go. Now prod between thumb and forefinger. This is how a medium steak should feel.

3. Well done Clench your fist tightly and prod between thumb and forefinger. The muscle feels much firmer; this is how well-done meat should feel.

INGREDIENTS

4 x 100–150g (3½–5½oz)
steaks, preferably fillet,
approx. cm (1in) thick, at
room temperature

1 tbsp olive oil

salt and freshly ground
black pepper

1 tsp cayenne pepper

1 tbsp Dijon mustard

1 tbsp soft light brown
sugar

PLAN OF ACTION!

1 COOK STEAKS → **2** ADD GLAZE → **3** FINISH UNDER GRILL

STEAK GLAZED WITH MUSTARD AND BROWN SUGAR

A simple, piquant steak makes for a super-speedy week-night meal. You can quickly throw together a tomato salad while the steaks are cooking, or if you've got a little more time, bake some sweet potato wedges to serve on the side.

SERVES 4 • READY IN 15 mins

1 SEASON AND COOK THE STEAKS

Rub the steaks with the oil and season well with salt, pepper, and cayenne pepper. Fry or chargrill over a high heat until cooked to your liking. For rare, allow 2–3 minutes each side; for medium, 3–4 minutes each side; and for well done, 4–5 minutes each side. Allow the meat to rest on a warmed plate for 3–5 minutes.

2 ADD THE GLAZE

Meanwhile, preheat the grill on its highest setting. Brush each steak on 1 side with a thin layer of mustard, then sprinkle with an even layer of the sugar.

3 FINISH UNDER THE GRILL

Grill the steaks for a minute or 2 only, until the sugar has melted and caramelized over the top. You don't want to cook them any further, just enough to create a lovely glazed effect.

FOOD FOR FRIENDS
WITHOUT THE FUSS

CITRUS-MARINATED OLIVES

Serve these zesty olives alongside dips and flatbreads for your guests to dig in. Make this a few days in advance to allow the flavours of the olives, fruits, spices, and herbs to mingle and infuse.

SERVES 6–8 • **READY IN** 12 mins, plus marinating

INGREDIENTS

- 1 tsp fennel seeds
- ½ tsp cumin seeds
- 250g (9oz) pitted black or green olives, or a mix of both
- grated zest of ½ orange
- grated zest of ½ lemon
- 2 garlic cloves, finely chopped
- 2 tsp chilli flakes, crushed
- 1 tsp dried oregano
- 1 tbsp lemon juice
- 1 tbsp red wine vinegar
- 2 tbsp olive oil
- 1 tbsp finely chopped flat-leaf parsley

1 TOAST THE SEEDS

Toast the fennel and cumin seeds in a dry pan over a low heat for 2 minutes, until aromatic.

2 MARINATE THE OLIVES

Combine the olives, toasted seeds, citrus zests, garlic, chilli flakes, oregano, lemon juice, vinegar, and oil and toss to coat the olives well. Place in an airtight container. Leave to marinate at room temperature for at least 8 hours.

3 SHAKE AND GARNISH

Shake the container occasionally to coat the ingredients while marinating. Stir in the parsley up to 3 hours before serving, and serve at room temperature.

TIP – Warming the olives will intensify the flavours of this dish. If you have time, gently heat them in a frying pan for about 5 minutes, until warmed through, and serve warm.

PLAN OF ACTION! **1** TOAST SEEDS → **2** MARINATE OLIVES → **3** SHAKE AND GARNISH

FIG AND GOAT'S CHEESE TOASTS

These toasts combine the freshness of figs with creamy soft goat's cheese and aromatic honey. A great combo for the perfect summer mezze dish.

SERVES 6 • **READY IN 20 mins**

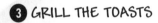

INGREDIENTS

- 1 baguette
- 8 ripe figs
- 250g (9oz) fresh creamy goat's milk cheese
- 6–8 tbsp clear rosemary or lavender honey

❶ TOAST THE BAGUETTE

Preheat the grill. Half the baguette lengthways and slice each half into smaller pieces. Arrange them in one layer on a baking tray and lightly toast them on both sides under the grill.

❷ TOP WITH FIGS AND CHEESE

Slice the figs lengthways. Arrange on top of the toasted baguette slices. Spoon over the goat's cheese, pressing it down a little.

❸ GRILL THE TOASTS

Place under the grill for 3–4 minutes until bubbling and a little golden.

❹ DRIZZLE AND SERVE

Drizzle with the honey and serve immediately.

> As an alternative to rosemary or lavender honey, use plain runny honey and sprinkle the toasts with your herb of choice.

PLAN OF ACTION!

❶ TOAST BAGUETTE → ❷ TOP WITH FIGS AND CHEESE → ❸ GRILL TOASTS → ❹ DRIZZLE AND SERVE

DIPS ON THE DOUBLE

Coriander jalapeño hummus

Blend I can of **haricot beans** with I tbsp **tahini**, I **jalapeño** (deseeded), **onion, coriander, olive oil, lime juice, garlic,** and **chilli flakes.**

You can substitute **black-eyed beans** for the black beans in this dip.

Black bean dip

Blend I can of **black beans** (drained) with **red onion, lime juice, olive oil, garlic, hot smoked paprika,** and **coriander.**

Sun-dried tomato dip

Whizz I jar of **sun-dried tomatoes** (including the oil) with **onion, garlic, olive oil, balsamic vinegar, basil,** and **dried oregano.**

Sweet potato hummus

Whizz I cooked **sweet potato** with ½ can of **chickpeas,** I tbsp **tahini, red onion, garlic, olive oil,** and **salt.**

Dips are great for when you've got friends over. The quantities here serve 4 as an appetizer, so adjust as needed. Allow ½–1 onion and 1–2 garlic cloves (crushed) per dip, and season to taste. Use a food processor to whizz the dips on page 166 into a paste; the recipes on this page can be chopped or mashed by hand with a knife or fork.

Spinach artichoke dip

Use a knife to finely chop the olives, anchovies, and capers before adding the wet ingredients, or use a food processor to whizz all the ingredients into a paste.

Tapenade

Mix a couple of handfuls of fresh **spinach** (wilted and drained) with a jar of **artichokes** (drained), 115g (4oz) each of **cream cheese**, and **soured cream**, grated **Parmesan**, **chilli flakes**, **salt**, and **garlic powder**.

Finely chop or whizz 1 jar of pitted **black olives** (drained), a few **anchovies**, and **capers** with **garlic**, **basil**, **olive oil**, and **lemon juice**.

Traditional guacamole

To serve, drizzle over **chilli sauce**.

Smoked fish dip

Mash together 3 **avocados** with **lime juice**, **salt**, **cayenne pepper**, and **chilli flakes**. Fold in **garlic**, chopped **cherry tomatoes**, and **coriander**.

Mix 2 fillets of flaked **smoked fish** with 115g (4oz) **cream cheese**, 1 tbsp **mayo**, and **lemon juice**. Fold in chopped **celery**, **jalapeño**, **gherkin**, **onion**, and **parsley**.

DIPPERS AND SNACK HACKS

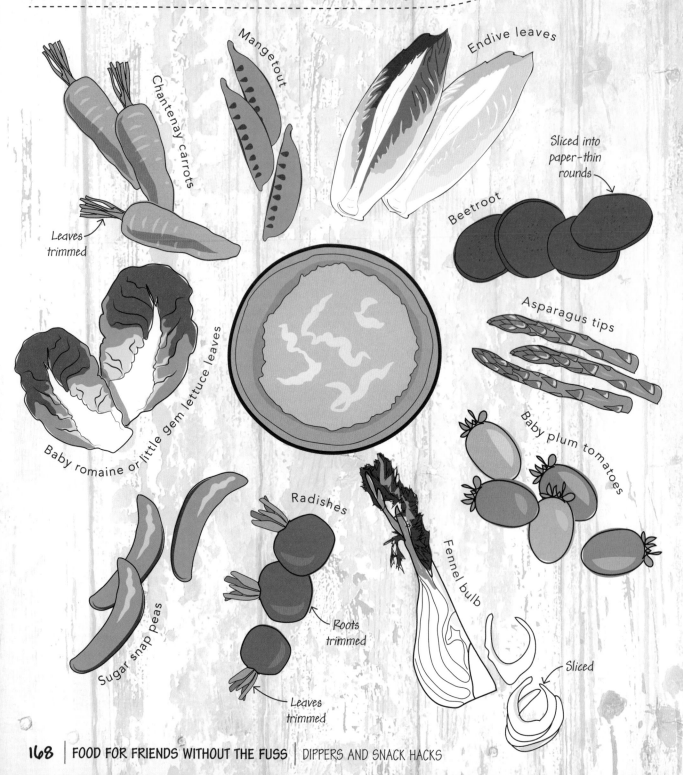

Mangetout

Endive leaves

Chantenay carrots

Sliced into paper-thin rounds

Beetroot

Leaves trimmed

Asparagus tips

Baby romaine or little gem lettuce leaves

Baby plum tomatoes

Radishes

Fennel bulb

Roots trimmed

Sugar snap peas

Sliced

Leaves trimmed

Now you've made your delicious dips (see pp166–7) – what to serve them with? The no-cook crudités on page 168 make for an impressive platter, while the snack hacks below are the perfect homemade alternative to shop-bought bites. They're sure to keep your guests happy!

Crostini

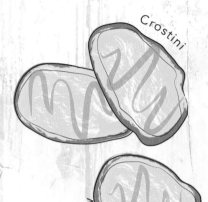

Preheat the oven to 180°C (350°F/Gas 4). Cut a baguette into slices, brush them with olive oil, then season with salt and pepper. Bake for 10–15 minutes, or until golden.

Herbed flatbread crisps

Preheat the oven to 200°C (400°F/Gas 6). Make a dough (see pp152–3, steps 1–4) and roll it out very thinly on a clean, flour-dusted surface. Brush with olive oil, scatter over dried herbs, and cut into segments. Transfer to a baking sheet, then bake for about 10 minutes, or until lightly browned.

Mixed root tempura also make great dippers! See pp178–9.

Preheat the oven to 180°C (350°F/Gas 4). Spoon heaped tablespoons of grated Parmesan cheese into mounds on a baking sheet lined with greaseproof paper. Bake for 8–10 minutes, or until golden brown and slightly toasted. Transfer to a wire rack to cool.

Why not try serving breadsticks wrapped in Parma ham alongside your homemade dippers? See pp188–9.

Parmesan thins

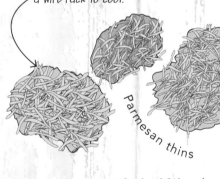

Tortilla chips

Preheat the oven to 200°C (400°F/Gas 6). Brush both sides of some corn tortillas with vegetable oil, then cut into triangles. Arrange in a single layer on a baking sheet, and bake for 7–8 minutes, or until golden and crispy. Serve sprinkled with salt.

Preheat the oven to 190°C (375°F/Gas 5). Slice your choice of sweet potatoes, parsnips, beetroot, or potatoes as thinly as possible (use a mandolin slicer, if you have one). Toss the vegetables with olive oil, and bake for 15–20 minutes, or until crisp. Serve sprinkled with salt.

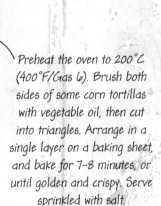

Vegetable crisps

FRIED HALLOUMI

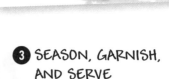

10 MINS OR LESS!

Halloumi is a firm, slightly springy white cheese traditionally made from sheep and goat's milk. It's salty-savoury flavour pairs well as a mezze with harissa paste, hummus, or a green salad with red onion.

SERVES 4-6 • **READY IN 8-10 mins**

INGREDIENTS

- 2 x 250g packets halloumi cheese
- flour, for dusting
- 120ml (4fl oz) olive oil, plus extra for drizzling
- 2 handfuls of thyme or oregano leaves
- juice of 2 lemons
- 1 lemon, cut into wedges, to serve

1 PREPARE THE HALLOUMI

Rinse the halloumi cheese before using to rid it of excess salt; dry well on kitchen paper. Cut the halloumi into 1cm (½in) thick slices and dust lightly with flour.

2 FRY THE HALLOUMI

Heat the oil in a non-stick frying pan over a high heat and fry the cheese for 2–3 minutes on each side, or until golden brown.

3 SEASON, GARNISH, AND SERVE

Remove from the pan and sprinkle with the thyme and lemon juice. Serve immediately with a little oil drizzled over and lemon wedges on the side.

Halloumi goes well with many dishes. You could try it with salsa criolla (see p146), inside a bun with a bean burger (see p100), or in place of goat's cheese in a bulgur wheat and pepper salad (see p99).

PLAN OF ACTION! **1** PREPARE HALLOUMI → **2** FRY HALLOUMI → **3** SEASON, GARNISH, AND SERVE

MOROCCAN-STYLE PRAWNS

Originally from Morocco, this easy dish tastes as good as it smells. Serve tapas-style with wooden cocktail sticks or forks, perhaps with some crème fraîche for dipping.

SERVES 4-6 • **READY IN** 10 mins

INGREDIENTS

- 500g (1lb 2oz) uncooked shelled large prawns (defrosted if frozen)
- 4 tbsp olive oil
- ½ tsp harissa paste or hot paprika
- 1 tsp ground ginger
- 1 tsp ground cumin
- ½ tsp ground coriander
- 3 garlic cloves, crushed
- 1 tbsp snipped flat-leaf parsley
- 1 tbsp snipped coriander

1 PREPARE THE PRAWNS
Drain the prawns on a double layer of kitchen paper.

2 FRY THE GARLIC AND SPICES
Heat the oil in a large frying pan, tip in the spices and garlic, and stir for a minute to release the flavours.

3 COOK THE PRAWNS
Add the prawns and cook for 1–2 minutes over a medium-high heat until they turn a little pink, then turn over. Cook until the prawns are pink all over, stirring frequently.

4 GARNISH AND SERVE
Stir in the fresh parsley and coriander and serve hot.

TIP – To prepare an unshelled, uncooked prawn, pull off the head, then carefully peel away the shell, starting from the underside. Discard both, or use for stock. Next, remove the dark vein. Lay the prawn flat and, using a small, sharp knife, make an incision down the back of the prawn and pull out the vein. Repeat for the remaining prawns and follow the method from step 1. Always wash your hands before and after preparing prawns, and thoroughly clean any kitchen equipment used.

PLAN OF ACTION!
 PREPARE PRAWNS → **FRY GARLIC AND SPICES** → **COOK PRAWNS** → 4 **GARNISH AND SERVE**

QUICK PICKLES

These are the homemade equivalent of gherkins, with a crunchier texture and punchier taste. They're delicious served as a side, or with charcuterie or cheese.

MAKES 2 jars • **READY IN** 10 mins, plus sterilizing and chilling

SPECIAL EQUIPMENT 2 x 200ml (7fl oz) jars

- 50g (1¾oz) caster sugar
- 2 tsp salt
- 200ml (7fl oz) white wine vinegar or rice wine vinegar
- freshly ground black pepper
- 4–5 small ridge cucumbers or 1 large cucumber, thinly sliced
- 1 tbsp finely chopped dill fronds
- ½ tsp dill seeds, lightly crushed

STERILIZE THE JARS

It's **important** to sterilize the jars so that your pickles don't become contaminated and turn mouldy. Allow the jars to cool before you fill them.

1 HEAT JARS

GLASS JARS

BAKING SHEET

Wash the jars, place them upside-down on a baking sheet, and put in an oven, preheated to 140°C (275°F/ Gas 1), for at least 15 minutes.

boiling water

METAL BOWL

2 BOIL LIDS

Pour boiling water over the lids and leave for 5 minutes. Remove and drain.

MAKE THE VINEGAR MIX

sugar

salt

black pepper

vinegar

WHISK

3 COMBINE

Whisk the sugar and salt with a little vinegar until dissolved. Add the remaining vinegar and a good grinding of black pepper.

PACK INTO JARS

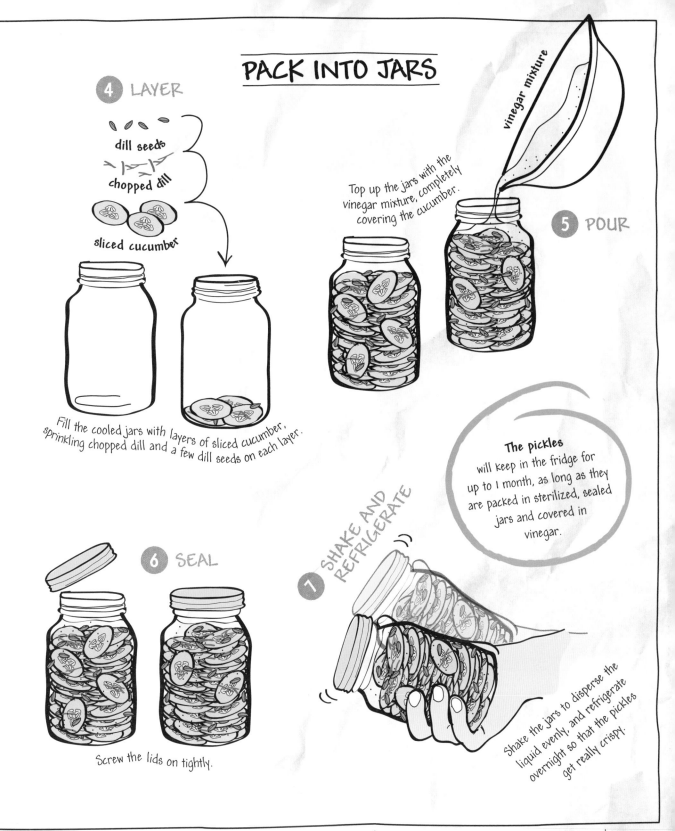

4 LAYER

dill seeds

chopped dill

sliced cucumber

Fill the cooled jars with layers of sliced cucumber, sprinkling chopped dill and a few dill seeds on each layer.

Top up the jars with the vinegar mixture, completely covering the cucumber.

vinegar mixture

5 POUR

The pickles
will keep in the fridge for up to 1 month, as long as they are packed in sterilized, sealed jars and covered in vinegar.

6 SEAL

Screw the lids on tightly.

7 SHAKE AND REFRIGERATE

Shake the jars to disperse the liquid evenly, and refrigerate overnight so that the pickles get really crispy.

THE PERFECT CHEESEBOARD

THE CHEESES

It's important to provide a range of flavours and textures to tickle the tastebuds and keep everyone happy – try some out first to find your favourites! Allow around 60g (2oz) of each cheese per person, and serve at room temperature.

1 MILD-TASTING
Edam is a semi-soft cheese with a sweet, buttery flavour.
Try also: Gouda, Taleggio, Jarlsberg, or Wensleydale.

2 STRONG-TASTING
Stilton is a smooth-textured, sharp-tasting blue cheese.
Try also: Roquefort, Gorgonzola, or Bleu d'Auvergne.

3 SOFT
Camembert is a soft white cheese with a creamy texture.
Try also: Brie, Brillat-Savarin, chèvre, or Stinking Bishop.

4 HARD
Manchego has the nutty taste of aromatic ewe's milk.
Try also: Cheddar, Emmental, Caerphilly, or pecorino.

THE ACCOMPANIMENTS

The right accompaniments will bring out the flavours of your cheeses, as well as cleansing the palate between mouthfuls.

5 CHUTNEY/JAM/PRESERVES
Try: **fig jam**, **runny honey**, red onion chutney, or plum chutney.

6 NUTS
Try: **smoked almonds**, cashews, or pickled walnuts.

7 FRESH FRUIT
Try: **apples**, pears, grapes, figs, or redcurrants.

8 PICKLES
Try: **cornichons**, gherkins, pickled onions, or piccalilli.

9 SPREAD/RELISH
Try: **olive tapenade** (see p167), or damson or quince paste.

10 BREADS
Try: **sourdough bread**, crackers, biscuits, or oat cakes.

When assembling your cheeseboard, aim for a carefully balanced selection of cheeses and accompaniments. This will give your guests lots of choice and allow them to create their own favourite combinations. If you're including a cheeseboard as part of a full meal, serve it after the main course, but before dessert.

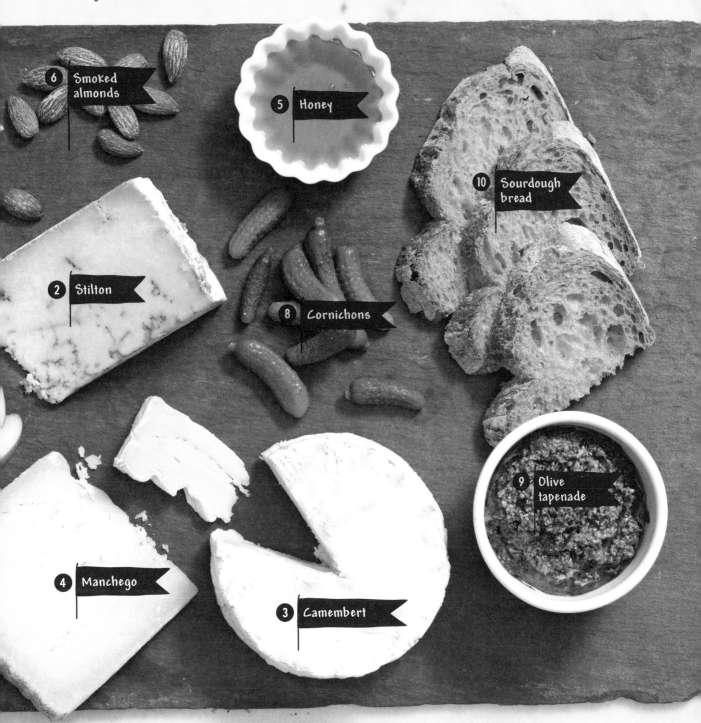

6 Smoked almonds

5 Honey

10 Sourdough bread

2 Stilton

8 Cornichons

9 Olive tapenade

4 Manchego

3 Camembert

SPEEDY SEAFOOD CEVICHE

Ceviche is a sophisticated-looking dish to serve to your guests as a starter or light snack. This brief, light pickling of raw fish brings out its natural flavours by "cooking" it with lemon juice – make sure you use only the freshest fish!

SERVES 4 • **READY IN** 20 mins, plus chilling

- -

1 SLICE THE FISH

With a sharp knife, cut the fish into small, evenly sized cubes.

2 PREPARE THE MARINADE

Spread the onion evenly in the bottom of a shallow, non-metallic dish. Pour over the lemon, or lime, juice and olive oil, then sprinkle with the pimentón and chilli.

3 ADD THE FISH

Place the fish on the onion, gently turning to coat with the marinade. Cover and marinate in the refrigerator for 15–20 minutes. Season, sprinkle with parsley, and serve with crusty bread.

TIP – The fish will be much easier to slice if you put it in the freezer for a few minutes first. The ceviche can be assembled, covered, and chilled up to 2 hours in advance. Return it to room temperature before serving.

Use extremely fresh semi- or firm-fleshed fish in ceviche. Salmon (shown here), halibut, turbot, monkfish, and sea bass all work well.

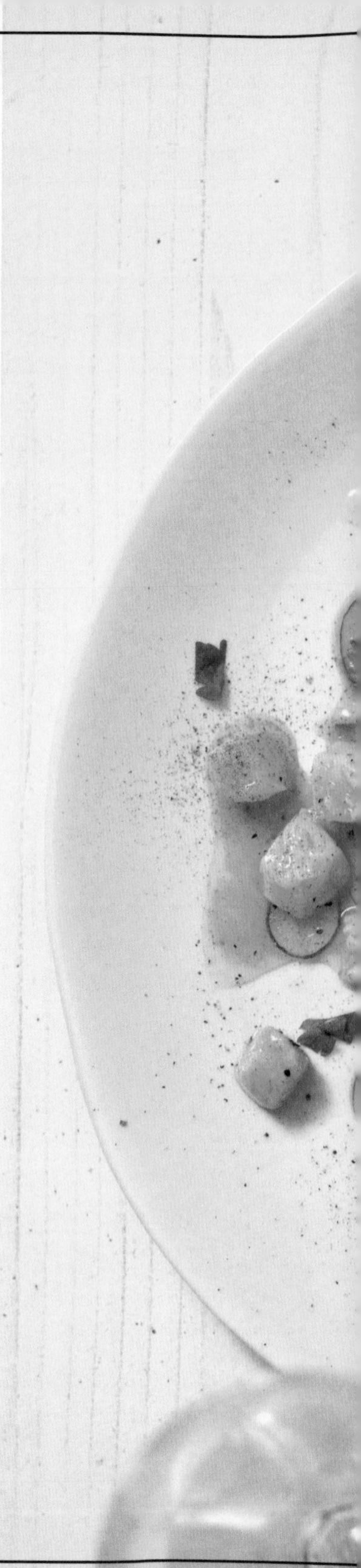

PLAN OF ACTION!

1 SLICE FISH → 2 PREPARE MARINADE → 3 ADD FISH

INGREDIENTS

450g (1lb) very fresh, semi- or firm-fleshed fish fillets, pinboned, skinned, and chilled

1 red onion, diced

juice of 2–3 lemons or limes

1 tbsp olive oil

½ tsp hot smoked paprika (pimentón picante)

1 chilli, finely chopped

salt and freshly ground black pepper

2 tbsp finely chopped flat-leaf parsley

MIXED ROOT TEMPURA

Root vegetables and leeks are given a Japanese treatment in this quick tempura recipe. Serve to your guests with sweet chilli sauce for dipping.

SERVES 4-6 • **READY IN 20-25 mins**

- 1 parsnip, cut into short fingers
- ½ small swede
- ½ small celeriac, cut into small chunks
- 1 large carrot, cut into short fingers
- 1 leek, cut into thick slices
- 2 tbsp cornflour
- sunflower oil, for deep-frying

FOR THE BATTER
- 85g (3oz) self-raising flour
- 85g (3oz) cornflour
- 200ml (7fl oz) sparkling mineral water
- 2 tsp sunflower oil
- ½ tsp salt
- ¾ tsp cumin seeds

PREPARE THE VEGETABLES

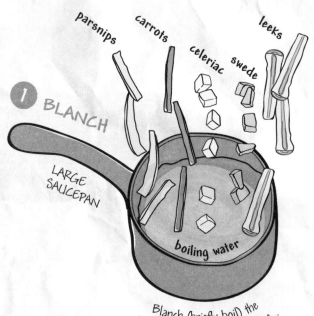

parsnips   carrots   celeriac   swede   leeks

1 BLANCH

LARGE SAUCEPAN

boiling water

Blanch (briefly boil) the vegetables for about 2 minutes...

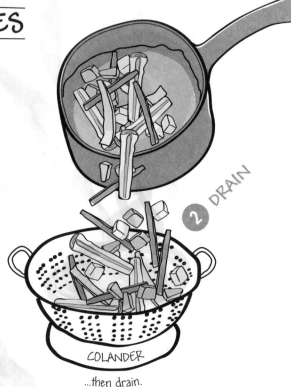

2 DRAIN

COLANDER

...then drain.

③ DRY

KITCHEN PAPER

④ COAT

cornflour

Sprinkle over the cornflour and toss to coat.

WHILE YOU FINISH PREPARING THE VEG, HEAT THE OIL IN A LARGE WOK OVER A HIGH HEAT.

MAKE THE BATTER

⑤ WHISK

cornflour

cumin seeds

sunflower oil

sparkling water

salt

self-raising flour

Whisk the batter ingredients until well combined.

⑥ DIP

Dip the veg in the batter, a few at a time, to coat lightly. Shake off any excess.

DEEP FRY IN BATCHES

LARGE WOK

⑦ FRY

sizzling hot oil

Deep-fry the veg for 2–3 minutes, turning occasionally, until golden.

SLOTTED SPOON

⑧ DRAIN AND SERVE

KITCHEN PAPER

Remove the tempura and drain. Serve hot with dipping sauce.

THE BRUSCHETTA BAR

Sauté the **mushrooms** with a little **butter** and **balsamic vinegar** over a high heat for 2 minutes, or until browned.

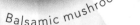

Balsamic mushrooms with cream cheese

Cream cheese, cucumber, and cherry tomato with snipped chives

For lots of **pesto recipe** ideas, see p136.

Pesto with shavings of Parmesan cheese

Ricotta cheese, raspberries, and honey with fresh mint

Wow your guests with a sumptuous selection of bruschetta toppings. Serve these classic Italian appetizers buffet-style, letting your guests help themselves. For the bases, drizzle thin slices of baguette with olive oil and grill or griddle until crisp on both sides.

Freshly ground **black pepper**

Tomato, mozzarella, and fresh basil

Chopped pitted olives and preserved red peppers with creamy goat's cheese

Diced mango and avocado with fresh coriander

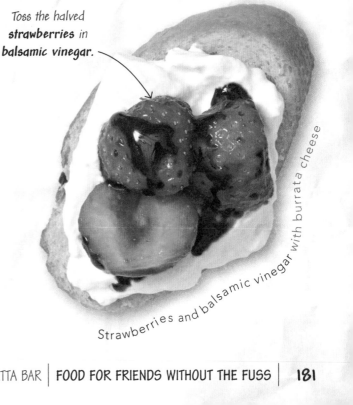

Toss the halved **strawberries** in **balsamic vinegar**.

Strawberries and balsamic vinegar with burrata cheese

INGREDIENTS

400g (14oz) ready-made puff pastry

2 tbsp red pesto

3 medium tomatoes, sliced

2–3 tbsp harissa paste (optional)

1 tbsp olive oil

100g (3½oz) feta cheese

few sprigs of fresh thyme, leaves picked

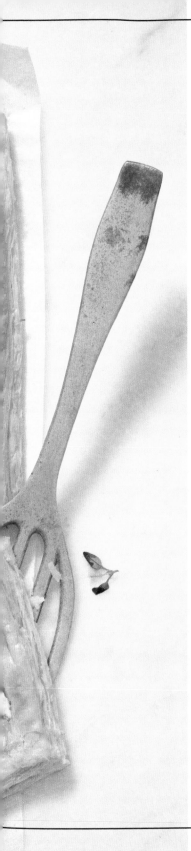

FETA, TOMATO, AND RED PESTO TART

This is a stylish-looking meal that's easy to whip up while your guests are chatting over drinks and nibbles, and it's suitable for vegetarians, too. For a finishing touch, try serving it with rocket on top or a green salad on the side.

SERVES 6 • **READY IN** 20 mins

1 PREPARE THE PASTRY

Preheat the oven to 200°C (400°F/ Gas 6). Roll out the pastry on a floured work surface, into a large rectangle or square. Lay on a baking tray, then use a sharp knife to score a border about 5cm (2in) in from the edges all the way around, being careful not to cut all the way through the pastry. Next, using the back of the knife, score the pastry around the outer edges – this will help it to puff up.

2 ASSEMBLE THE TART

Working inside the border, smother the pastry with the pesto. Arrange the tomatoes on top, cut-side up. Mix the harissa, if using, with the olive oil, and drizzle over the tomatoes. Crumble over the feta cheese and scatter with the thyme leaves.

3 BAKE TO PERFECTION

Bake the tart in the oven for about 15 minutes, or until the pastry is cooked and golden. Serve hot.

You can have fun mixing and matching lots of different toppings for this tart. Why not try adding anchovies, olives, or preserved artichokes? Basil works well instead of thyme, and chilli or garlic oil can be used in place of harissa. Also, if you've made your own pesto (see pp136–37), this tart is ideal for showing it off!

POTSTICKER DUMPLINGS

These Chinese-style dumplings are pan-fried for a browned, crunchy exterior and then steamed to cook the filling. Serve with soy sauce or sweet chilli sauce.

MAKES 36 • **READY IN** 20–30 mins

- 36 wonton wrappers
- 1 tsp sesame oil
- plain flour, for dusting

FOR THE FILLING
- 450g (1lb) minced pork
- 100g (3½oz) cabbage, shredded
- 100g (3½oz) onion, finely chopped
- 50g (1¾oz) fresh root ginger, finely chopped
- 100g (3½oz) spring onions, chopped
- 3 garlic cloves, crushed
- 2 tsp sesame oil
- 1 tbsp hoisin sauce
- 2 tbsp rice wine

For a veggie filling, use 400g (14oz) finely chopped shiitake mushrooms instead of the pork, omit the onion and ginger, halve the amount of spring onions and sesame oil, and add a tsp of salt and 50g (1¾oz) finely chopped coriander.

MAKE THE FILLING

1 COMBINE

cabbage · onion · root ginger · spring onions · crushed garlic · sesame oil · hoisin sauce · rice wine

minced pork

Place all the ingredients for the filling in a large bowl and mix well to combine.

FORM THE DUMPLINGS

dusting of flour

2 FILL

Fill with mixture

wonton wrappers

Lay the wonton wrappers on a lightly floured surface. Place 1 tablespoon of the filling in the centre of each wrapper.

3 FOLD AND SEAL

water

Use your finger to dampen the edges of the wrappers with water.

Fold the wrappers in half, over the filling, to form a triangle.

Use your fingers to press and seal the edges together.

FRY, STEAM, AND SERVE

4 FRY

Heat the oil over a medium heat.

LARGE NON-STICK FRYING PAN

Add the dumplings, in batches, and fry for 1–2 minutes on each side, until browned.

5 STEAM

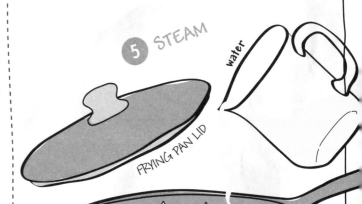

water

FRYING PAN LID

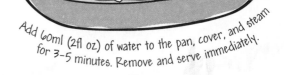

Add 60ml (2fl oz) of water to the pan, cover, and steam for 3–5 minutes. Remove and serve immediately.

To save time, prepare the dumplings in batches, forming the second batch while the first is cooking, and so on.

DEVILLED EGGS

These easy-to-prepare boiled eggs with spiced yolks are great crowd-pleasers. Just serve them at your next party or take them on a picnic, and watch them disappear!

SERVES 4 • **READY IN** 18 mins

INGREDIENTS

- 6 eggs
- 1 tsp mustard
- 1 tsp hot paprika, plus extra for dusting
- 3 tbsp mayonnaise
- salt and freshly ground black pepper
- 3 cherry tomatoes, cut in quarters
- 1 tbsp chopped chives

❶ BOIL THE EGGS

Place the eggs in a large saucepan and cover with plenty of water. Bring to the boil, then turn down the heat and simmer for about 8 minutes. Carefully remove the eggs and plunge them into cold water, leaving them to cool. Peel off the shells and cut the eggs in half lengthways.

❷ MAKE THE YOLK MIXTURE

Remove the yolks and place them in a bowl. Add the mustard, paprika, and mayonnaise, and mash together with a fork until well combined. Season to taste with salt and pepper.

❸ FILL THE EGG WHITES AND SERVE

Divide the yolk mixture between the egg white halves and top each one with a slice of cherry tomato. Sprinkle over the chives, dust with paprika, and serve cold.

Instead of the cherry tomatoes, serve with a range of toppings, such as chopped olives, smoked salmon, bacon bits, or sun-dried tomatoes.

 PLAN OF ACTION! **BOIL EGGS** ⟶ **MAKE YOLK MIXTURE** ⟶ **FILL EGGS AND SERVE**

QUICHE CUPS

These individual quiches are quick and easy to make and are ideal finger food for parties, buffets, and picnics. You'll need a food processor to make short work of the pastry dough and a 12-hole muffin tin to bake the cups in. The quantities given here are for 12 quiche cups.

HOW TO MAKE

- 115g (4oz) unsalted butter, chilled and diced, plus extra for greasing
- 225g (8oz) plain flour
- 1 tsp sugar
- 1 tsp salt
- 6 eggs, beaten
- 250ml (9fl oz) milk

Preheat the oven to 180°C (350°F/ Gas 4) and grease the muffin tin.

For the pastry, place the butter, flour, sugar, and salt in a food processor and pulse until the mixture resembles breadcrumbs. Add 4 tablespoons of cold water, a little at a time, and bring together to form a dough. Divide the dough and firmly press it into the muffin tin to create a thin crust.

For the filling, place the eggs and milk in a bowl and whisk well to combine. Add the filling (try any of the combinations, right, or experiment with your own) and mix well to combine. Pour the filling into the muffin tin and bake for about 20 minutes, or until the pastry is golden and the egg set. Best served hot.

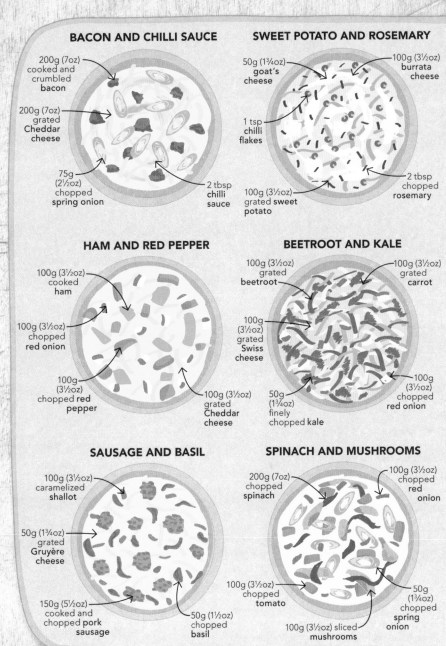

BACON AND CHILLI SAUCE
- 200g (7oz) cooked and crumbled bacon
- 200g (7oz) grated Cheddar cheese
- 75g (2½oz) chopped spring onion
- 2 tbsp chilli sauce

SWEET POTATO AND ROSEMARY
- 50g (1¾oz) goat's cheese
- 100g (3½oz) burrata cheese
- 1 tsp chilli flakes
- 100g (3½oz) grated sweet potato
- 2 tbsp chopped rosemary

HAM AND RED PEPPER
- 100g (3½oz) cooked ham
- 100g (3½oz) chopped red onion
- 100g (3½oz) chopped red pepper
- 100g (3½oz) grated Cheddar cheese

BEETROOT AND KALE
- 100g (3½oz) grated beetroot
- 100g (3½oz) grated carrot
- 100g (3½oz) grated Swiss cheese
- 50g (1¾oz) finely chopped kale
- 100g (3½oz) chopped red onion

SAUSAGE AND BASIL
- 100g (3½oz) caramelized shallot
- 50g (1¾oz) grated Gruyère cheese
- 150g (5½oz) cooked and chopped pork sausage
- 50g (1½oz) chopped basil

SPINACH AND MUSHROOMS
- 200g (7oz) chopped spinach
- 100g (3½oz) chopped red onion
- 100g (3½oz) chopped tomato
- 100g (3½oz) sliced mushrooms
- 50g (1¾oz) chopped spring onion

THE PERFECT CHARCUTERIE BOARD

A charcuterie board is the ideal pre-supper fare – great for relaxed, tapas-style snacking alongside drinks. If you include a cheeseboard (see pp174–5), too, you can make the whole meal a sharing experience.

THE MEATS

Pork offers the widest range of cured cuts (although other meats are cured, too). Choose 3 or 4 different meats in total, allowing 3 slices of each meat per person.

1 DRY-CURED MEATS
Aim for a selection of 2–3 dry-cured meats, such as:
Serrano ham – a Spanish "mountain" ham with a sweet taste and chewy texture.
Coppa (or capocollo or capicola) – a well-marbled Italian ham made from pork shoulder or neck.
Parma ham (or prosciutto di Parma) – a famous Italian ham that's sweet, salty, and moist.
Try also: Ibérico ham, bellota, or speck.

2 DRY-CURED SAUSAGES
Include 1–2 dry-cured sausages, such as:
Dry-cured chorizo – a rich Spanish sausage spiced with hot or sweet smoked paprika.
Try also: salchichón, saucisson sec, or salami.

THE ACCOMPANIMENTS

Offer a good selection of accompaniments. Pairing the meats with a range of other tastes and textures will make for interesting flavour combinations.

3 PÂTÉS AND TERRINES
These cooked meats bring a unique texture to the board.
Try either **chicken liver pâté**, pork rillettes, or Brussels pâté.

4 SWEET AND SAVOURY SPREADS
Include 1–2 sweet spreads, such as **peach jam** or **comb honey**, and 1 savoury spread, such as **Dijon** or wholegrain mustard.

5 OLIVES AND PICKLES
Pickled vegetables are a must. Include 2–3, such as **green olives**, **pickled onions**, **gherkins**, or pickled okra.

6 SALAD LEAVES AND HERBS
A simple green salad offers a light and fresh counterpoint to the other strong flavours. Try: **rocket**, mixed baby leaves, or fresh dill.

7 BREADS
Provide an array of breads and crackers, such as **crispbreads**, **breadsticks**, and slices of baguette.

4 Peach jam

3 Chicken liver pâté

4 Dijon mustard

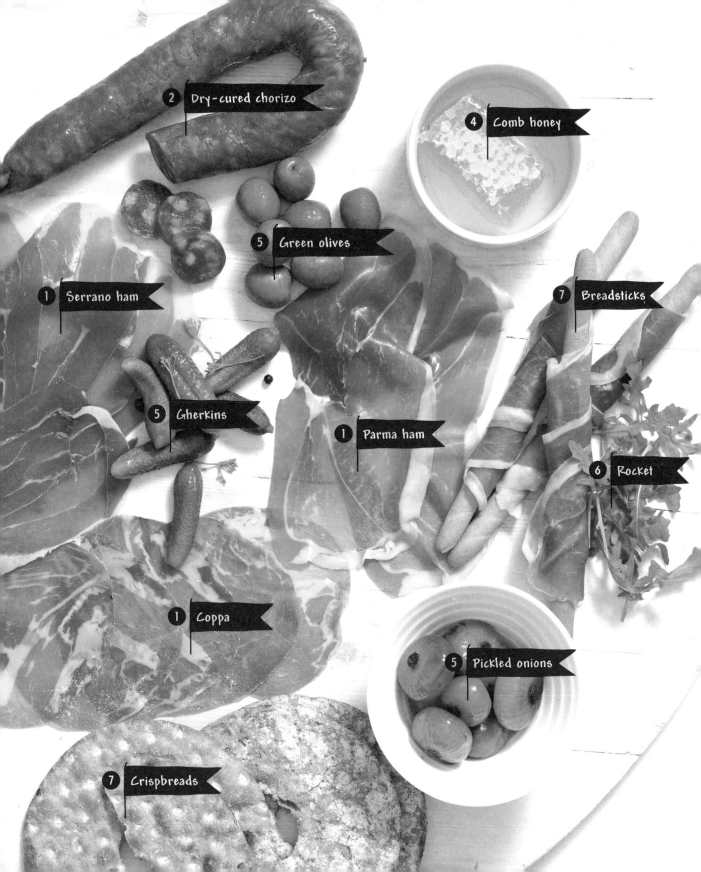

2 Dry-cured chorizo

4 Comb honey

5 Green olives

1 Serrano ham

7 Breadsticks

5 Gherkins

1 Parma ham

6 Rocket

1 Coppa

5 Pickled onions

7 Crispbreads

SMOKED SALMON AND CRÈME FRAÎCHE SPAGHETTI

A simple yet stylish way to pull together a fabulous supper with just a few ingredients, this straightforward spaghetti is packed with flavour – dill and salmon are a match made in heaven!

SERVES 4 • **READY IN 15 mins**

INGREDIENTS

- 300g (10oz) dried spaghetti
- salt and freshly ground black pepper
- 200ml (7fl oz) half-fat crème fraîche
- 115g (4oz) smoked salmon, finely chopped
- 1 tbsp finely chopped capers, rinsed, or more to taste
- finely grated zest of ½ lemon
- 2 tbsp finely chopped dill
- finely grated Parmesan cheese, to serve

① COOK THE PASTA

Cook the pasta in a large pan of boiling salted water according to the packet instructions.

② MIX THE CRÈME FRAÎCHE AND SALMON

Meanwhile, beat the crème fraîche in a bowl until smooth. Add the smoked salmon, capers, lemon zest, and dill, and season to taste.

③ TOSS, HEAT, AND SERVE

Drain the pasta (reserving a ladleful of the cooking water) and return it to the pan with the reserved water. Toss the sauce through the pasta and return it to the heat, stirring just long enough both for the pasta to soak up some of the sauce and for the sauce to heat through. Loosen the sauce with the reserved cooking water if necessary. Serve with the Parmesan cheese.

PLAN OF ACTION! ① COOK PASTA → ② MIX CRÈME FRAÎCHE AND SALMON → ③ TOSS, HEAT, AND SERVE

SAUTÉED SCALLOPS WITH PANCETTA

Treat your friends to a taste of the sea! Scallops are so quick to cook that you've got time to make a rich *jus* (sauce) from pancetta and balsamic vinegar. Serve with pasta or bread for a main meal.

SERVES 4 • **READY IN** 20 mins

INGREDIENTS

- 12 fresh scallops, with or without coral (see tip)
- salt and freshly ground black pepper
- 1–2 tbsp olive oil
- 115g (4oz) pancetta, diced
- dash of good-quality thick balsamic vinegar
- 2 handfuls of spinach leaves, stalks removed
- juice of 1 lemon

① FRY THE SCALLOPS

Pat the scallops dry using kitchen paper, and season with salt and pepper. Heat the oil in a non-stick frying pan over a medium-high heat. When hot, add the scallops, positioning them around the edge of the pan. Sear for 1–2 minutes on one side, then turn them over, starting with the first one you put in the pan. Once you have completed the circle, remove the scallops from the pan (again starting with the first one), and set aside to keep warm.

② COOK THE PANCETTA AND MAKE THE SAUCE

Cook the pancetta in the same pan and cook for 2–3 minutes, or until crispy. Add a generous amount of balsamic vinegar to the pan, increase the heat to high, and allow it to boil for 2–3 minutes, stirring to deglaze the pan. Then drizzle the sauce over the cooked scallops.

③ WILT THE SPINACH

Still using the same pan, tip in the spinach. Cook for 2–3 minutes, moving it around the pan, until it is just wilted. Squeeze over the lemon juice, and serve immediately with the scallops and pancetta sauce.

TIP – Buy your scallops out of the shell to save time – they're available pre-prepared at most large supermarkets and fish counters. You may still need to remove the coral – it's an edible part of the scallop that's usually red and soft, that some people prefer not to eat. If you'd prefer your scallops without the coral, trim it off before cooking using a sharp knife.

PLAN OF ACTION!
① FRY SCALLOPS → ② COOK PANCETTA AND MAKE SAUCE → ③ WILT SPINACH

MOULES MARINIÈRES

This classic French dish is a delicious meal to share with friends – you can eat this with your hands, using the empty shells to scoop out the mussel meat.

SERVES 4 • **READY IN** 20 mins

- 60g (2oz) butter
- 2 onions, finely chopped
- 3.6kg (8lb) fresh mussels, cleaned
- 2 garlic cloves
- 600ml (1 pint) dry white wine
- 4 bay leaves
- 2 sprigs of thyme
- salt and freshly ground black pepper
- 2–4 tbsp chopped parsley
- crusty bread, to serve

PREPARE THE MUSSELS

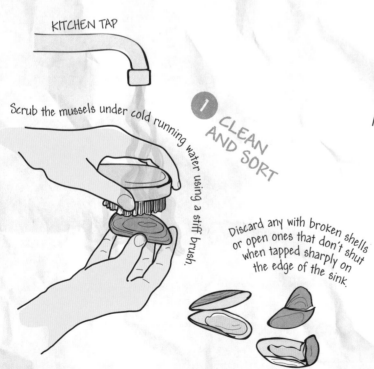

KITCHEN TAP

Scrub the mussels under cold running water using a stiff brush.

1 CLEAN AND SORT

Discard any with broken shells or open ones that don't shut when tapped sharply on the edge of the sink.

SHARP KNIFE

2 DEBEARD AND RINSE

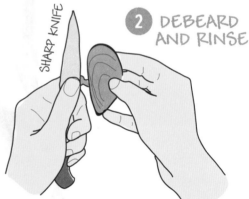

Pull off the "beards" by tugging each beard sharply away from the shell. Then rinse again.

Mussel "beards"
are fibrous threads that mussels use for gripping onto surfaces. They are inedible, so it's important to remove them.

COOK THE DISH

3 SOFTEN

LARGE
SAUCEPAN

butter and onions

Heat the butter over a medium heat.
Gently fry the onion until softened.

4 COMBINE

salt

pepper

garlic

bay leaves

mussels

thyme

wine

Add the mussels, garlic, wine,
bay leaves, thyme, salt, and pepper.
Increase the heat and bring to the boil.

5 COVER AND COOK

Shake the pan occasionally.

Cover and cook for 5 minutes.

6 GARNISH AND SERVE

parsley

Discard any closed mussels and stir
in the chopped parsley. Serve straight
away with chunks of crusty bread.

THAI FISHCAKES

You can serve these spicy fishcakes as a starter with a bowl of sweet chilli sauce for everyone to dip into, or add cooked noodles tossed with sesame oil, finely sliced spring onions, and soy sauce to make this into a satisfying main course.

SERVES 4 • **READY IN** 20 mins
SPECIAL EQUIPMENT Food processor

1 WHIZZ THE INGREDIENTS TO A PASTE

Place all the ingredients except the egg, seasoning, and oil in a food processor, and whizz to a rough paste, scraping down the sides once or twice. Add the egg and plenty of salt and pepper, and whizz again.

2 FLATTEN MIXTURE IN THE PAN

Heat a little of the oil in a large frying pan over a medium-high heat. Scoop up 1 tablespoon of the mixture, then carefully slide it into the pan and flatten slightly; it should be about 2cm (¾in) thick. Repeat until all the mixture has been used, but do not crowd the pan (you may need to cook in batches, adding more oil as needed).

3 FRY THE FISHCAKES

Shallow-fry for 1 or 2 minutes on each side until golden, turning carefully. Transfer to a plate lined with kitchen paper. Serve hot with a drizzle of sweet chilli sauce, wedges of fresh lime juice, and wild rocket leaves.

TIP – You can use pre-prepared and cooked prawns (fresh or frozen), but make sure that frozen prawns are thoroughly defrosted first.

Try making miniature versions of these for an easy canapé. You can make them up to 1 day in advance, storing them in an airtight container in the fridge. Just reheat them in a hot oven until piping hot before serving.

INGREDIENTS

300g (10oz) cooked, shelled, and deveined prawns

3 garlic cloves, peeled, but left whole

small handful of coriander leaves

2 hot red chillies, deseeded

splash of Thai fish sauce, such as nam pla

splash of dark soy sauce

small handful of basil leaves

juice of 2 limes, plus lime wedges to serve

1 egg

salt and freshly ground black pepper

3–4 tbsp vegetable or sunflower oil

sweet chilli sauce, to serve

wild rocket leaves, to serve

INGREDIENTS

8 tbsp soy sauce

8 tbsp Chinese rice wine
or dry sherry

6 tbsp thinly sliced fresh
root ginger

4 small sea bass, gutted
and rinsed

2 tbsp sesame oil

1 tsp salt

4 spring onions, trimmed
and thinly sliced

8 tbsp sunflower oil

4 garlic cloves, chopped

2 small red chillies,
deseeded and thinly sliced

zest of 2 limes

small handful of chopped
coriander leaves, to serve

PLAN OF
ACTION!

1 MAKE
SAUCE

2 SEASON
FISH

3 PREPARE
FOR STEAMING

4 STEAM
FISH

CHINESE-STYLE STEAMED BASS

This bright dish is sure to impress your friends with minimal effort. Serve with white basmati rice or Vietnamese glass noodles for a healthy, speedy meal that wouldn't look out of place on a restaurant table.

SERVES 4 • **READY IN** 20 mins
SPECIAL EQUIPMENT Two-tier steamer or large steaming rack

- -

❶ MAKE THE SAUCE

Prepare a two-tier steamer, or position a large steaming rack in a wok with water so it doesn't touch the water. Bring to the boil. Stir together the soy sauce, rice wine, and 4 tbsp ginger, and set aside.

❷ SEASON THE FISH

Using a sharp knife, make slashes in the fish, 2.5cm (1in) apart and not quite as deep as the bone, on both sides. Rub the fish inside and out with the sesame oil and salt.

❸ PREPARE FOR STEAMING

Scatter one-quarter of the spring onions over a heatproof serving dish that will hold 2 fish and fit in one of the tiers of the steamer. Place 2 fish on the dish and pour over half the sauce. Repeat with the remaining fish, using a second serving dish. If using a steaming rack, use a heatproof serving dish large enough to hold all 4 fish.

❹ STEAM THE FISH

Place the dishes in the steamer or the large dish on the rack, cover, and steam for 10–12 minutes, or until the fish is cooked through and flakes easily when tested with a knife. Remove the fish, cover, and keep warm.

❺ GARNISH AND SERVE

Meanwhile, heat the sunflower oil in a small saucepan over a medium-high heat until shimmering. Scatter the fish with the remaining spring onions and ginger, and the garlic, chilli, and lime zest. Drizzle the hot oil over the fish and serve with the chopped coriander.

TIP – To save time, ask your fishmonger to gut the sea bass for you.

ON THE GRILL

Scallops, peach, and red onion

Prawns, red pepper, pineapple, and red onion

Pork, pineapple, and red onion

Salmon fillet pieces, red and green peppers, and onion

MARINATE IN...

1 part each of **olive oil** and **lemon juice**.

4 parts **soy sauce**, 2 parts **water**, and 1 part each of **brown sugar** and **red chilli**.

3 parts **honey**, 2 parts **lime juice**, and 1 part **cayenne pepper**.

4 parts **hoisin sauce**, 1 part each of **honey**, **lime juice**, crushed **garlic**, and finely chopped **root ginger**, and **chilli flakes** to taste.

Allow these mouthwatering skewers to marinate for 1 hour, if you have time, or simply coat generously and grill straight away. If you're using wooden skewers, soak them in cold water for at least 30 minutes before grilling, to prevent them from burning.

Garlic and lemon prawns

Chicken, red and yellow peppers, mushrooms, and bacon

Beef fillet, cherry tomatoes, and baby potatoes

Diced halloumi, green and yellow courgettes, and yellow pepper

2 parts **olive oil**, 1 part each of **lemon juice** and crushed **garlic**, and **salt** and **black pepper** to taste.

5 parts **brown sugar**, 2 parts **cumin**, and 1 part **chilli flakes**.

1 part each of **olive oil**, balsamic vinegar, and finely chopped fresh **rosemary**.

3 parts each of **olive oil** and finely chopped fresh **green herbs**, and 2 parts **lemon juice**.

A MEDLEY OF DIPPING SAUCES

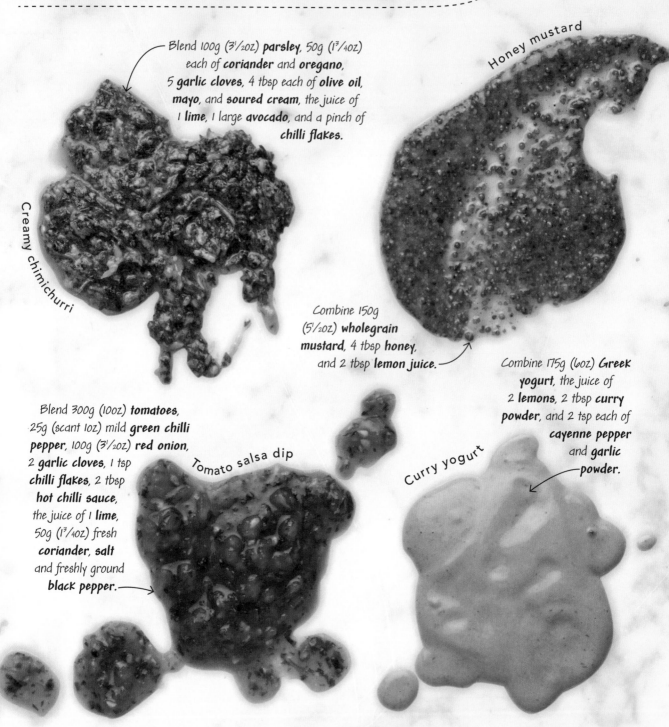

Blend 100g (3½oz) **parsley**, 50g (1¾oz) each of **coriander** and **oregano**, 5 **garlic cloves**, 4 tbsp each of **olive oil**, **mayo**, and **soured cream**, the juice of 1 **lime**, 1 large **avocado**, and a pinch of **chilli flakes**.

Honey mustard

Creamy chimichurri

Combine 150g (5½oz) **wholegrain mustard**, 4 tbsp **honey**, and 2 tbsp **lemon juice**.

Combine 175g (6oz) **Greek yogurt**, the juice of 2 **lemons**, 2 tbsp **curry powder**, and 2 tsp each of **cayenne pepper** and **garlic powder**.

Blend 300g (10oz) **tomatoes**, 25g (scant 1oz) mild **green chilli pepper**, 100g (3½oz) **red onion**, 2 **garlic cloves**, 1 tsp **chilli flakes**, 2 tbsp **hot chilli sauce**, the juice of 1 **lime**, 50g (1¾oz) fresh **coriander**, **salt** and freshly ground **black pepper**.

Tomato salsa dip

Curry yogurt

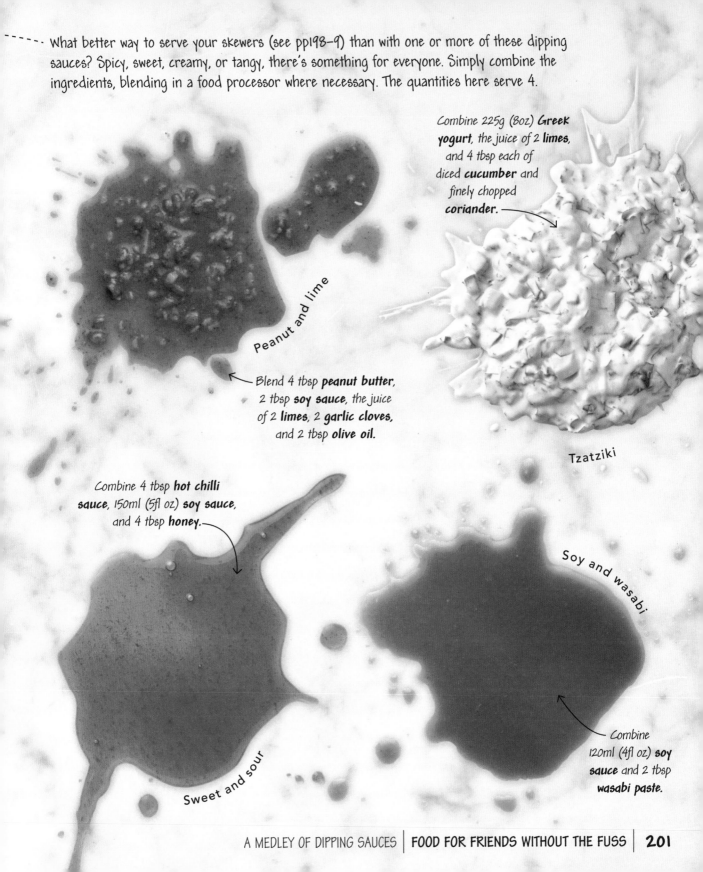

What better way to serve your skewers (see pp198–9) than with one or more of these dipping sauces? Spicy, sweet, creamy, or tangy, there's something for everyone. Simply combine the ingredients, blending in a food processor where necessary. The quantities here serve 4.

Combine 225g (8oz) **Greek yogurt**, the juice of 2 **limes**, and 4 tbsp each of diced **cucumber** and finely chopped **coriander**.

Peanut and lime

Blend 4 tbsp **peanut butter**, 2 tbsp **soy sauce**, the juice of 2 **limes**, 2 **garlic cloves**, and 2 tbsp **olive oil**.

Tzatziki

Combine 4 tbsp **hot chilli sauce**, 150ml (5fl oz) **soy sauce**, and 4 tbsp **honey**.

Soy and wasabi

Combine 120ml (4fl oz) **soy sauce** and 2 tbsp **wasabi paste**.

Sweet and sour

SEARED DUCK WITH RASPBERRY SAUCE

Seriously impress your guests with this stylish dish, ready in less than half an hour! Tangy raspberry sauce and rich crispy duck are divine together – add wilted, buttery spinach and creamed potatoes to make a more substantial meal.

SERVES 4 • **READY IN** 20 mins

❶ SCORE THE SKIN

Use a sharp knife to score the skin on the duck breasts. Rub the meat generously with salt and pepper.

❷ FRY THE DUCK BREASTS

Place the duck skin-side down in a heavy-based frying pan over a medium-low heat. Allow the duck fat to render (melt) for 10–12 minutes. Turn and cook for a further 3–5 minutes on the other side. Set aside to rest. Keep warm.

❸ MAKE THE SAUCE

While the duck is cooking, melt the butter in a separate pan. Add the sugar and shallots and cook until caramelized. Press the raspberries through a sieve to ensure a smooth sauce. Add the raspberry pulp, cardamom, and vinegar to the pan. Cook, stirring frequently, for 5–7 minutes.

❹ PLATE UP AND SERVE

Transfer the duck to a serving plate and serve topped with the raspberry sauce.

TIP – To prepare the cardamom, split the pods open with a knife point and scrape the seeds out. Discard the pods and crush the seeds into a powder using a pestle and mortar or, if you don't have one, using the end of a rolling pin and a sturdy mixing bowl.

① **SCORE SKIN**	→ ② **FRY DUCK**	→ ③ **MAKE SAUCE**	→ ④ **PLATE UP AND SERVE**

INGREDIENTS

600g (1lb 5oz) skin-on
duck breasts

salt and freshly ground
black pepper

FOR THE SAUCE
1 tbsp butter

1 tbsp brown sugar

100g (3½oz) shallots,
finely chopped

200g (7oz) fresh
raspberries, deseeded and
roughly chopped

4 cardamom pods, seeds
removed and crushed

1 tbsp red wine vinegar

PORK STEAKS WITH FRIED APPLES

This dish allows you to feed your guests in style just minutes after they arrive. The sweet, caramelized apples provide a quick and tasty accompaniment to the salty pork, and the creamed spinach adds a flash of iron-rich greenery.

SERVES 4 • **READY IN** 20 mins

1 COOK THE PORK

Season the pork well with salt, pepper, and chilli flakes. Heat 1 tablespoon of the oil in a large frying pan and fry the pork for 3–5 minutes on each side, depending on the thickness, until cooked through. Set it aside, loosely covered in foil to keep it warm while it rests.

2 PREPARE THE APPLES

Add the remaining 1 tablespoon of oil and the butter to the pan and allow them to bubble up. Add the apple pieces, pour the lemon juice over, sprinkle with the sugar, and season with salt and pepper.

3 CARAMELIZE THE APPLES

Cook the apples over a medium heat for 5–7 minutes, turning occasionally, until they soften and start to caramelize. Turn them gently using 2 spatulas, so the pieces don't break up.

4 WILT THE SPINACH

Meanwhile, make the creamed spinach. Melt the butter and oil in a separate large, deep-sided frying pan. Cook the garlic for 1 minute, then add the baby spinach. Turn it through the oil and sauté it for 2–3 minutes, until cooked through. Add the cream, season well, bring to a boil, and reduce. Serve alongside the pork steaks, each one topped with one-quarter of the apples.

Steps

1. **COOK PORK** →
2. **PREPARE APPLES** →
3. **CARAMELIZE APPLES** →
4. **WILT SPINACH**

INGREDIENTS

4 x 100g (3½oz) boneless pork steaks

salt and freshly ground black pepper

1 tsp chilli flakes

2 tbsp olive oil

1 tbsp butter

4 small apples, peeled, cored, and quartered

1 tbsp lemon juice

½ tsp light brown sugar

FOR THE CREAMED SPINACH

1 tbsp butter

1 tbsp olive oil

1 small garlic clove, crushed

400g (14oz) baby spinach leaves

100ml (3½fl oz) double cream

salt and freshly ground black pepper

HARISSA-SPICED LAMB CHOPS

Spice up some lamb chops with Moroccan-inspired seasoning, add mashed chickpeas and chopped tomatoes tossed with olive oil and balsamic vinegar, and you've got a tasty feast on the table in less than half an hour.

SERVES 4 • **READY IN** 20 mins

1 GRILL THE CHOPS

Preheat the grill on its medium setting. Place the chops on a foil-lined baking tray and grill on one side for 8 minutes.

2 MAKE THE RUB

While the chops are grilling, place the breadcrumbs, zest, harissa, coriander, and olive oil in a bowl, season, and stir well to combine evenly.

3 SEASON THE CHOPS

Turn the chops when ready, and press the breadcrumb and harissa mixture onto the uncooked side of each chop. Grill for a further 8 minutes.

4 COOK THE CHICKPEAS

Meanwhile, make the chickpea mash. Heat the oil in a saucepan over a medium heat, add the onion, and fry for 5 minutes. Add the garlic and cook for 2 minutes. Stir in the chickpeas, lemon juice, and extra virgin olive oil, and gently heat.

5 MAKE THE MASH

Remove from the heat and mash roughly with a potato masher; it should not be smooth. Stir in the coriander and season generously. Serve the chops with the chickpea mash and a dressed tomato salad.

TIP – Make the breadcrumb topping up to 3 days ahead, cover, and store in an airtight container in the fridge.

1. GRILL CHOPS → 2. MAKE RUB → 3. SEASON CHOPS → 4. COOK CHICKPEAS → 5. MAKE MASH

INGREDIENTS

8 x 100g (3½oz) lamb loin chops

50g (1¾oz) fresh white breadcumbs

finely grated zest of 1 lemon

1 tbsp harissa paste

2 tbsp finely chopped coriander leaves

2 tsp olive oil

salt and freshly ground black pepper

FOR THE CHICKPEA MASH

1 tbsp olive oil

1 red onion, finely chopped

2 garlic cloves, finely chopped

2 x 400g cans chickpeas, drained and rinsed

1½ tbsp lemon juice

2 tbsp extra virgin olive oil

2 tbsp finely chopped coriander leaves

tomato salad, to serve

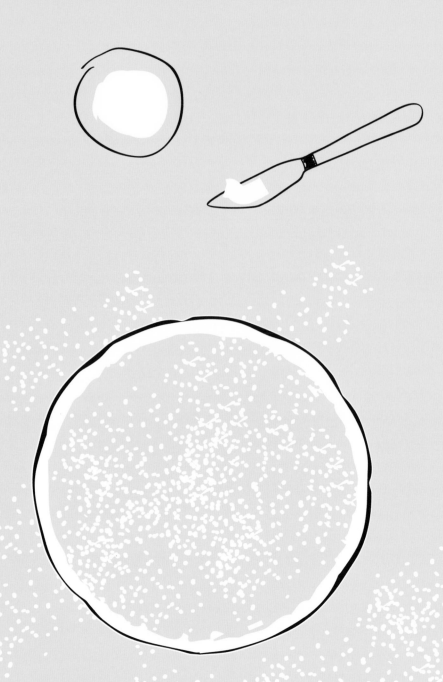

SHORT AND SWEET

FRESH ORANGES WITH CARAMEL AND PASSION FRUIT

Add homemade caramel and zingy passion fruit to your oranges to lift this fruit-bowl staple to a whole new level! Throw on fresh mint leaves and chopped pistachios, and serve with Greek yogurt for a colourful, refreshing dessert.

SERVES 4 • **READY IN** 15 mins

- -

❶ MAKE THE CARAMEL

Put the sugar in a saucepan with 2 tablespoons of cold water. Stir, then heat gently without stirring, until the sugar melts. Boil rapidly until the sugar syrup turns a rich golden brown. Remove from the heat and add another 2 tablespoons of cold water. Stir over a gentle heat until the caramel dissolves, then leave to cool.

❷ PREPARE THE ORANGES

Slice off the top and bottom from each orange, discard, then place the oranges on a chopping board. Carefully slice off the skin and pith, leaving as much flesh as possible, and following the sides of the orange so you keep the shape of the fruit. Slice the oranges horizontally into thin strips, discarding any pips as you come across them. Arrange the orange slices on a serving platter. Pour over any remaining juice.

❸ DRIZZLE AND DECORATE

Drizzle the caramel over the orange slices and sprinkle over the cinnamon. Slice the passion fruit in half, scoop out the seeds and scatter with the pistachios, if using. Decorate with the mint leaves and serve.

PLAN OF ACTION!

1 MAKE CARAMEL → **2** PREPARE ORANGES → **3** DRIZZLE AND DECORATE

INGREDIENTS

60g (2oz) sugar

4 oranges

good pinch of ground cinnamon

seeds from 2 passion fruit

small handful of chopped pistachios (optional)

handful of mint leaves, to decorate

MIXED BERRIES WITH WHITE CHOCOLATE SAUCE

10 MINS OR LESS!

A refreshing and luxurious recipe, this pudding pairs a warm and rich sauce with sweet, frozen fruit – a great way to use up that packet of berries in the freezer!

SERVES 4 • **READY IN** 10 mins

INGREDIENTS

- 125g (4½oz) good-quality white chocolate, plus extra to serve (optional)
- 140ml (4½fl oz) double cream or whipping cream
- 450g (1lb) packet frozen mixed berries, such as raspberries, strawberries, blackberries, and redcurrants

① MELT THE CHOCOLATE

Break the chocolate into pieces and place in a saucepan over a low heat. Add the cream and bring almost to the boil, stirring constantly, until the chocolate has melted and the mixture is well combined.

② ARRANGE AND SERVE

Divide the berries among 4 serving dishes. Pour over the chocolate mixture and serve topped with grated white chocolate, if you like.

PLAN OF ACTION!

① MELT CHOCOLATE

② ARRANGE AND SERVE

LYCHEES WITH GINGER AND STAR ANISE

The subtle and fragrant aniseed flavour of the star anise goes well with the refreshing lychees and ginger in this quick and cooling dessert.

SERVES 4 • **READY IN** 10 mins, plus marinating

INGREDIENTS

- 2 tbsp ginger syrup
- 400ml can lychees, drained and 2 tsp juice reserved
- 1 star anise
- 2 balls stem ginger, finely diced
- Greek yogurt, to serve

① MIX THE SYRUP AND JUICE

Place the ginger syrup and reserved lychee juice in a small bowl and mix well to combine.

② ARRANGE THE DISH

Place the lychees and star anise in a glass dish. Scatter over the ginger and drizzle with the ginger syrup and lychee juice mixture.

③ CHILL AND SERVE

Chill in the fridge for 30 minutes, or longer if you have the time, for the flavours to develop. Divide between serving glasses and serve topped with Greek yogurt.

PLAN OF ACTION! ① MIX SYRUP AND JUICE → ② ARRANGE DISH → ③ CHILL AND SERVE

WARM FRUIT COMPÔTE

This dish is ideal for autumn and winter, when supplies of fresh fruit are limited; it's a sweet, spiced dessert that's sure to warm you up on a cold day. Serve with yogurt on the side and runny honey drizzled over, if you like.

MAKES 10   •   **READY IN** 15–20 mins

- -

1 STEW THE FRUIT

Melt the butter in a heavy saucepan over a medium heat. Add the fruit and cinnamon stick. Cook gently, stirring often, until the fruit has completely softened.

2 STIR IN THE SUGAR

Stir in the sugar and heat for a further couple of minutes, or until the sugar has dissolved.

3 SPRINKLE WITH LEMON JUICE AND SERVE

Remove the pan from the heat, sprinkle with lemon juice, and serve warm with a spoonful of yogurt and a drizzle of honey.

TIP – The compôte can be made up to 3 days in advance, covered, and refrigerated.

For convenience, keep a bag of frozen cherries in the freezer and use instead of the prunes and apricots in the compôte. It will cut down the preparation time. Any leftover compôte is delicious with granola (see pp30–33).

PLAN OF ACTION!

1. STEW FRUIT → 2. STIR IN SUGAR → 3. SPRINKLE WITH LEMON JUICE

INGREDIENTS

30g (1oz) butter

6 dried prunes, chopped

6 dried apricots, chopped

2 large apples, peeled, cored, and chopped

1 firm pear, peeled, cored, and chopped

1 cinnamon stick

2 tsp sugar

2 tsp lemon juice

yogurt and honey, to serve

ORANGE SORBET

Often served in restaurants as a refreshing palate cleanser between courses, sorbets also make lovely, light summer desserts.

SERVES 2 • **READY IN** 20 mins, plus cooling and freezing

SPECIAL EQUIPMENT Hand-held electric whisk

- 125g (4½oz) caster sugar
- 2 large oranges
- 1 tbsp orange-flower water
- 1 egg white

MAKE THE SYRUP

1 DISSOLVE

sugar

orange zest

VEGETABLE PEELER

WOODEN SPOON

SAUCEPAN

Dissolve the sugar in 300ml (10fl oz) of water over a gentle heat. Add the zest from the oranges and simmer for 10 minutes.

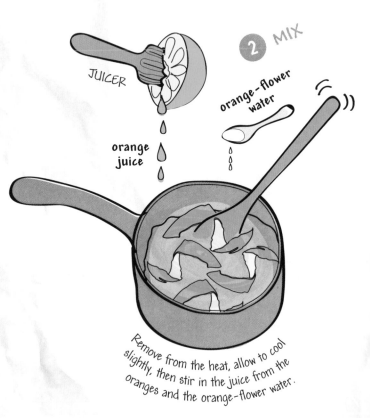

2 MIX

JUICER

orange juice

orange-flower water

Remove from the heat, allow to cool slightly, then stir in the juice from the oranges and the orange-flower water.

3 STRAN

SIEVE

PREPARE THE EGG WHITE

WHILE THE SYRUP IS COOLING, PREPARE THE EGG WHITE.

4 WHISK

ELECTRIC WHISK

SHALLOW CONTAINER

Strain the syrup, discarding the zest, and leave to cool completely.

Place the egg white in a bowl and whisk until soft peaks form.

COMBINE AND FREEZE

5 FOLD

SPATULA

FREEZERPROOF CONTAINER

Transfer the syrup to a freezerproof container and fold in the whisked egg white. Freeze for 4 hours, or until solid.

6 MASH

FORK

Mash with a fork to break up any ice crystals, then freeze again. To serve, leave to soften for 10–15 minutes.

INGREDIENTS

4 ripe bananas

1 tsp
vanilla extract

PLAN OF ACTION!

1 PEEL AND FREEZE → **2** WHIZZ IT UP → **3** EAT OR REFREEZE

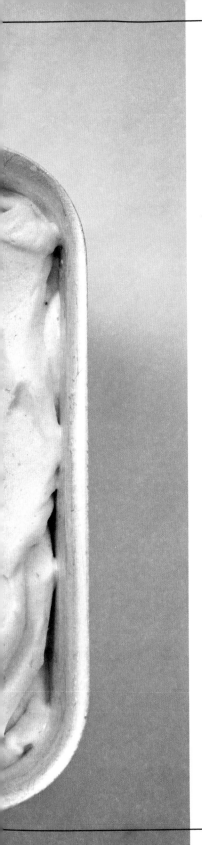

QUICK BANANA ICE CREAM

This is the quickest and easiest ice cream you will ever make – and it's super healthy, too! This dessert is a great way to use up any ripening bananas in your fruit bowl, and you don't even need an ice-cream maker.

SERVES 4 • **READY IN** 5 mins, plus freezing
SPECIAL EQUIPMENT Food processor

1 PEEL AND FREEZE

Simply peel the bananas, chop them into 2cm (¾in) chunks, and place them in a freezer container. Seal, and put in the freezer until frozen.

2 WHIZZ IT UP

When the bananas are frozen solid, process them in a food processor with the vanilla extract, until you have a smooth, thick ice cream. You may need to scrape down the sides a couple of times during the process.

3 EAT NOW OR REFREEZE

Either eat the softened banana ice cream immediately, or freeze for a few minutes for it to firm up once more before serving.

TIP – If you have ripening bananas that you can't use up quickly enough, peel them, cut into chunks, and freeze on a plate. When they are frozen solid, transfer to a freezer bag and add more bananas until you have enough to make this ice cream.

A few spoonfuls of chocolate and hazelnut spread, or smooth peanut butter, added to the food processor along with the bananas works well here, too.

A MONTH OF SUNDAES

*For the spice mix, combine 1 tbsp **ground cinnamon**, 2 tsp **ground ginger**, and ½ tsp each of **ground nutmeg**, crushed **cardamom seeds** and **ground cloves**.*

CHOCOLATE BROWNIE AND STRAWBERRIES

Chocolate brownie pieces, chocolate ice cream, halved strawberries, and whipped cream.

BANANA AND TOFFEE

Banana muffin or banana bread, vanilla ice cream, banana slices, and toffee sauce.

CHOCOLATE AND PEANUT BUTTER PRETZEL

Chopped pretzels, vanilla ice cream, melted peanut butter, and chocolate sauce.

PUMPKIN PIE-SPICED BLONDIE

Blondie brownie, vanilla ice cream, crumbled digestive biscuit, and pumpkin pie spice.

A sundae is the ideal speedy, decadent dessert – simply throw together a few key ingredients with some ice cream, drizzle with sauce or syrup, and serve in a beautiful glass to show off the layers! They are also a great way to turn brownies (see pp242–5) into an indulgent dessert.

Toss the **pineapple pieces** in **dark brown sugar**. Griddle for 7–10 minutes or until bubbling.

Toast the **coconut flakes** in a dry frying pan until they begin to brown at the edges.

You can substitute **toasted marshmallows** for the marshmallow fluff.

COCONUT AND GRIDDLED PINEAPPLE

Toasted **coconut flakes**, **coconut ice cream**, griddled **pineapple pieces**, **chocolate sauce**, and **whipped cream**.

GINGER SNAP AND PECAN

Crushed **ginger snaps**, **dulce de leche ice cream**, and **caramel sauce**.

MARSHMALLOW AND BANANA SPLIT

Vanilla ice cream, sliced **banana**, **marshmallow fluff**, and **chocolate sauce**.

GINGER AND DARK CHOCOLATE

Dark **chocolate** pieces, **vanilla ice cream**, stem **ginger** pieces (with the syrup from the jar), and crushed **walnuts**.

SHAKES AND FLOATS

SHAKES

GINGERBREAD SHAKE

Blend 2 scoops of vanilla ice cream, 500ml (16fl oz) milk, 1 tsp ground cinnamon, 1 tsp grated nutmeg, 1 tsp vanilla extract, and 2 tsp ground ginger. Garnish with crushed ginger snaps.

GRASSHOPPER SHAKE

Blend 2 scoops of mint chocolate chip ice cream, 1 tsp mint extract, 250ml (9fl oz) milk, and 250ml (9fl oz) chocolate milk. Garnish with mint thins and fresh mint leaves.

BANANA AND PEANUT BUTTER SHAKE

Blend 500ml (16fl oz) milk, 2 scoops of Quick Banana Ice Cream (see pp218–19), and 100g (3½oz) smooth peanut butter. Garnish with dried banana chips.

FROZEN STRAWBERRY SHAKE

Blend 250ml (9fl oz) milk, 250g (9oz) frozen strawberry yogurt, and 100g (3½oz) fresh strawberries, hulled. Garnish with slices of fresh strawberry.

A milkshake or float makes for a delicious, drinkable dessert that can be ready in a couple of minutes. For the shakes, use your preferred milk and whizz the ingredients in a blender. For the floats, pour in the fizzy drink first, let it settle, then pop in a scoop or two of ice cream or sorbet. These quantities make 2 tall glasses.

LEMONADE FLOAT

Divide 150ml (5fl oz) traditional lemonade and 350ml (12fl oz) lemon-and-lime soda between 2 glasses. Drop a scoop of lemon sorbet into each glass.

BERRY AND GINGER ALE FLOAT

Divide 500ml (16fl oz) ginger ale between 2 glasses. Drop a scoop each of blackcurrant sorbet and raspberry sorbet into each glass.

FLOATS

NEAPOLITAN FLOAT

Divide 500ml (16fl oz) soda water between 2 glasses. Drop a small scoop each of strawberry, chocolate, and vanilla ice cream into each glass. Drizzle strawberry sauce and chocolate sauce over each float.

CHERRY COLA FLOAT

Divide 500ml (16fl oz) cherry cola between 2 glasses. Drop a scoop each of chocolate ice cream and cherry ice cream into each glass. Drizzle chocolate sauce over each float.

INGREDIENTS

500ml (16fl oz)
double cream

1 tsp vanilla extract

2 tbsp caster sugar

150g (5½oz) ready-made
meringues

300g (10oz) strawberries,
chopped quite small

150g (5½oz)
raspberries

FOR THE FRUIT COULIS
150g (5½oz) strawberries
150g (5½oz) raspberries
50g (1¾ oz) caster sugar

10
MINS
OR LESS!

ETON MESS WITH WARM FRUIT COULIS

This is a crowd-pleasing, summery dessert that's very quick to make. Serve in sundae glasses or clean glass jars to show off the pretty red and white layers. For a lighter taste, try replacing the double cream with Greek yogurt.

SERVES 6 • READY IN 10 mins

1 WHISK THE CREAM

Whisk the cream until it is very stiff, then whisk in the vanilla extract and fold in the sugar.

2 BASH THE MERINGUES

Place the meringues in a freezer bag and bash with a rolling pin to break into uneven pebble-sized pieces. It's nice to have a mixture of large pieces and smaller crumbs, for the best texture.

3 COMBINE THE MIXTURE

Fold together the cream mixture, the meringues, and the fruit. Cover and chill while you make the coulis.

4 MAKE THE COULIS

Place the fruit for the coulis, sugar, and 3 tbsp of water into a small saucepan with a lid. Cover, place over a medium heat, and bring to a boil, then remove the lid, stir, and simmer the fruit for about 5 minutes, or until it is soft.

5 BLEND AND SERVE

Blend the fruit with a hand-held blender until smooth, then press it through a nylon sieve to remove all the seeds. Pour over the Eton mess while still warm.

For a tropical twist, substitute a peeled and sliced mango for the strawberries and raspberries, then use the flesh and seeds of a passion fruit to replace the coulis.

RASPBERRY CHEESECAKE

This fresh and light cheesecake requires no cooking and takes very little time to prepare. You can make it up to 24 hours ahead and chill until required.

SERVES 6 • **READY IN** 15 mins, plus chilling
SPECIAL EQUIPMENT 20cm (8in) round loose-bottomed flan tin

- 50g (1¾oz) unsalted butter
- 100g (3½oz) dark chocolate, broken into pieces
- 150g (5½oz) digestive biscuits
- 400g (14oz) mascarpone cheese
- grated zest and juice of 2 limes, plus extra zest for garnishing
- 2–3 tbsp icing sugar, plus extra for dusting
- 225g (8oz) raspberries

MAKE THE BASE

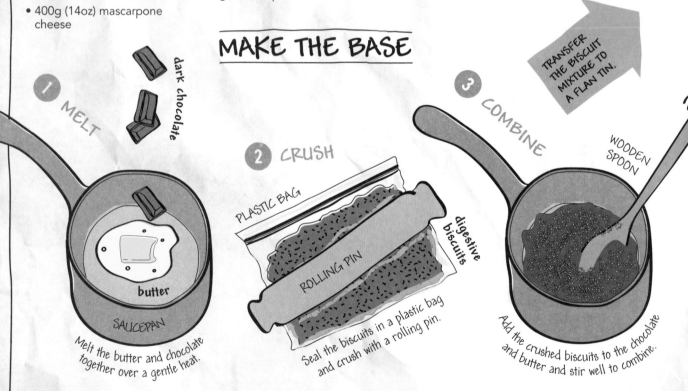

1 MELT
dark chocolate
butter
SAUCEPAN
Melt the butter and chocolate together over a gentle heat.

2 CRUSH
PLASTIC BAG
ROLLING PIN
digestive biscuits
Seal the biscuits in a plastic bag and crush with a rolling pin.

3 COMBINE
TRANSFER THE BISCUIT MIXTURE TO A FLAN TIN.
WOODEN SPOON
Add the crushed biscuits to the chocolate and butter and stir well to combine.

MAKE THE CHEESE MIXTURE

4 FORM

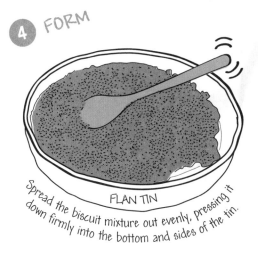

FLAN TIN

Spread the biscuit mixture out evenly, pressing it down firmly into the bottom and sides of the tin.

5 BEAT

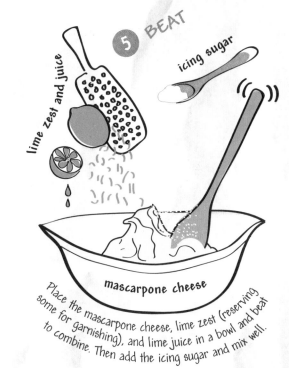

lime zest and juice

icing sugar

mascarpone cheese

Place the mascarpone cheese, lime zest (reserving some for garnishing), and lime juice in a bowl and beat to combine. Then add the icing sugar and mix well.

ASSEMBLE THE CAKE

6 SPREAD

Pour the cheese mixture over the biscuit base.

SPATULA

Spread the mixture out evenly and smooth over the top with a spatula. Chill in the fridge for 1 hour.

7 ARRANGE AND SERVE

Arrange the raspberries over the cheesecake, dust with icing sugar, and garnish with lime zest. Slice and serve.

INGREDIENTS

200g (7oz) caster sugar

175g (6oz) light corn syrup

125g (4½oz)
shelled pistachios

30g (1oz) butter, cut into
cubes, plus extra
for greasing

1 tsp bicarbonate of soda

1 tsp vanilla extract

PLAN OF ACTION!

1 HEAT SUGAR → **2** ADD PISTACHIOS → **3** STIR IN DRY INGREDIENTS

④
COOL
AND SMASH

PISTACHIO BRITTLE

Brittles are a simple, fun sweet that can be made quickly from storecupboard ingredients. You can dig into this cracked straight from the pan, or store it in an airtight container and keep it for a few days.

SERVES 6–8 • **READY IN** 20 mins, plus cooling
SPECIAL EQUIPMENT Sugar thermometer (see also "TIP", below)

❶ **HEAT THE SUGAR AND WATER**

In a heavy-based saucepan, combine the sugar, corn syrup, and 60ml (2fl oz) water over a medium heat. Cook, stirring frequently with a wooden spoon, until a sugar thermometer dipped into the liquid reads 160°C (325°F) and the sugar turns brittle and golden brown.

❷ **ADD THE PISTACHIOS**

At this stage, known as "hard breaking point", add the pistachios. Continue stirring until the temperature rises to 160°C (325°F) again.

❸ **STIR IN THE REMAINING INGREDIENTS**

Remove from the heat and stir in the butter, bicarbonate of soda, and vanilla extract. Continue to stir as it foams and the butter melts.

❹ **POUR, COOL, AND SMASH**

Pour onto a greased 23 x 35cm (9 x 14in) baking tray and let it cool completely. Break into pieces and store in an airtight container.

TIP – If you do not have a sugar thermometer, drop a small amount of the mixture into a glass of cold water – if it turns brittle and snaps, the mixture is hot enough.

Why not try combining different dried fruit and nuts to find your favourite combination? Peanuts are a classic and delicious addition.

PANNACOTTA

This simple Italian dessert is easy to prepare and makes a refreshing end to a meal, especially served with a fruit compôte (see p214) or a summery fruit coulis (see "tip", below).

SERVES 4 • **READY IN** 15 mins, plus setting
SPECIAL EQUIPMENT 4 x 150ml (5fl oz) ramekins

INGREDIENTS

- 400ml (14fl oz) single cream
- 250ml (9fl oz) whole milk
- 100g (3½oz) caster sugar
- 4 sheets of gelatine
- 1 tbsp sunflower oil
- fruit compôte, fruit coulis, or fruit salad, to serve
- crushed pistachio nuts, to serve

❶ HEAT THE CREAM AND MILK

Heat the cream and milk in a saucepan. When it is hot, but not boiling, pour it into a bowl and whisk in the sugar until dissolved.

❷ SOAK THE GELATINE

Meanwhile, soak the gelatine in a bowl of water for 5 minutes, squeeze out the excess, and add to the hot cream. Heat it very gently, stirring, until the gelatine dissolves.

❸ PREPARE AND FILL THE RAMEKINS

Rub the insides of four 150ml (5fl oz) ramekins with a piece of kitchen paper dipped in the oil. Divide the cream mixture between the ramekins, cover, and cool. Transfer to the fridge for at least 2 hours, or until the cream has set.

❹ TURN OUT AND GARNISH

To serve, fill a bowl with hot water and carefully dip the base of each ramekin into the water. Run a small knife around the edge of each ramekin, and turn the pannacottas out onto plates. Garnish with fruit compôte, fruit coulis, or a fruit salad, and a sprinkling of crushed pistachios.

TIP – You can make a fruit coulis while the pannacotta is setting. Put 3 tbsp of maple syrup, 3 tbsp of orange juice, and 225g (8oz) of halved strawberries in a pan, and simmer gently for 5 minutes. Remove from the heat and purée in a food processor or blender until smooth, or spoon through a sieve.

PLAN OF ACTION!   ❶ HEAT MILK AND CREAM → ❷ SOAK GELATINE → ❸ PREPARE AND FILL RAMEKINS → ❹ TURN OUT AND GARNISH

CARAMELIZED APPLE AND CHOCOLATE CRÊPES

Indulge in some paper-thin, French-style crêpes for an easy and delicious dessert. Make sure you use crisp apples, as these will keep their substance and texture better during cooking.

MAKES 4–6 • **READY IN** 20 mins, plus resting (optional)

INGREDIENTS

- 50g (1¾oz) plain flour
- salt
- 1 egg, lightly beaten
- 150ml (5fl oz) milk
- 150ml (5fl oz) double cream
- knob of butter
- 2–3 tbsp golden caster sugar, depending on the sweetness of the apples
- 4 pink-skinned eating apples, sliced
- vegetable oil
- 125g (4½oz) dark chocolate, grated

① MAKE THE BATTER

Sift the flour into a mixing bowl with a pinch of salt and make a well in the centre. Place the egg and a little of the milk in the well. Using a wooden spoon, gradually stir the egg mixture, letting a little of the flour fall in as you go and adding the rest of the milk a little at a time. When it is all incorporated, whisk the mixture with a balloon whisk to remove any lumps. Transfer to the fridge to rest for 15 minutes, if you have time.

② WHIP THE CREAM

Meanwhile, put the cream in a mixing bowl and whisk until lightly whipped, then set to one side.

③ CARAMELIZE THE APPLES

Put the butter and sugar in a frying pan over a low heat and stir until the sugar has dissolved. Add the apple slices and toss well. Cook for 5–10 minutes, or until caramelized, then put to one side and keep warm.

④ FRY THE CRÊPES

While the apples are caramelizing, fry the crêpes. Heat a pancake pan or small frying pan over a high heat. When hot, add a tiny amount of vegetable oil, then swirl it around the pan and pour it into a jug. Add 2 tablespoons of batter to the pan and swirl it around so it covers the base. Loosen the edges of the crêpe with a palette knife and cook for 1 minute, or until golden. Flip the crêpe and cook the other side for a minute or so. Slide onto a warmed plate and repeat until all the mixture has gone.

⑤ FILL, FOLD, AND SERVE

To serve, pile some of the caramelized apple slices and a dollop of cream onto each crêpe, fold, and top with plenty of chocolate shavings.

PLAN OF ACTION!   ① MAKE BATTER → ② WHIP CREAM →  ③ CARAMELIZE APPLES → ④ FRY CRÊPES → ⑤ FILL, FOLD, AND SERVE

CINNAMON CHURROS

These cinnamon- and sugar-sprinkled Spanish snacks are quick to make and will be devoured just as quickly! Try dipping them in this spicy chocolate sauce.

MAKES 20 • **READY IN** 20 mins, plus cooling
SPECIAL EQUIPMENT Piping bag • 2cm (¾in) star-shaped nozzle

- 25g (scant 1oz) unsalted butter
- 200g (7oz) plain flour
- 50g (1¾oz) caster sugar
- 1 tsp baking powder
- 1 litre (1¾ pints) peanut or sunflower oil
- 1 tsp ground cinnamon

- 150ml (5fl oz) double cream
- 1 tbsp caster sugar
- 1 tbsp unsalted butter
- pinch of salt
- ¼ tsp chilli powder or cayenne pepper, to taste

FOR THE CHOCOLATE CHILLI SAUCE

- 50g (1¾oz) good-quality dark chocolate, broken into pieces

MAKE THE BATTER

1 COMBINE

Sift together the flour and baking powder into a bowl, and add half the sugar.

2 STIR

HEAT-RESISTANT JUG

butter

Mix the butter with 200ml (7fl oz) of boiling water.

3 MIX

WOODEN SPOON

Beat the hot butter liquid and flour mixture together to form a thick paste.

PIPE AND FRY THE CHURROS

WHILE THE BATTER IS COOLING, HEAT THE OIL FOR DEEP-DRYING.

oil

cube of bread

4 HEAT

Pour the oil to a depth of 10cm (4in).

Heat the oil to 190°C (375°F). When it's hot enough, a cube of bread popped into the pan will turn golden brown in 1 minute.

5 PIPE

PIPING BAG

Meanwhile, spoon the cooled batter into a piping bag fitted with a star-shaped nozzle.

6 FRY AND DRAIN

SLOTTED SPOON

KITCHEN PAPER

Pipe 7cm (2¾in) lengths of the batter directly into the hot oil. Cook the churros in batches for 1–2 minutes on each side before leaving them to drain.

7 TOSS

PLATE

sugar and cinnamon

Toss the hot churros in the remaining sugar and the cinnamon.

MAKE THE SAUCE

Heat the sauce ingredients, except the chilli powder and salt, in a medium, heatproof bowl over a saucepan of barely simmering water. Stir constantly for 3–4 minutes until the sauce melds together, then add the salt and chilli powder.

8 MELT

double cream

chocolate

sugar

chilli powder

butter

HEATPROOF BOWL

SAUCEPAN

Make sure the bowl doesn't touch the water when you're making the sauce, otherwise it will become too hot and may burn and spoil.

FRESH FRUIT HAND PIES

HOW TO MAKE

MAKES 12-14

- 450g (1lb) plain flour, plus extra for dusting
- 230g (8oz) butter, chilled and diced
- 50g (1¾oz) brown sugar
- pinch of salt

Place all the ingredients in a food processor, add 60ml (2fl oz) of water, and whizz until a smooth dough forms. Cover in cling film and chill for 1 hour.

To form the pies, roll out the dough on a floured surface. Use a biscuit cutter or tumbler to cut 7.5-10cm (3-4in) wide circles. Place 1 tbsp of the filling on one half of each circle and fold over the other half to create a half-moon shape. Place on lined baking sheets and bake for 15-17 minutes at 180°C (350°F/Gas 4), or until golden brown.

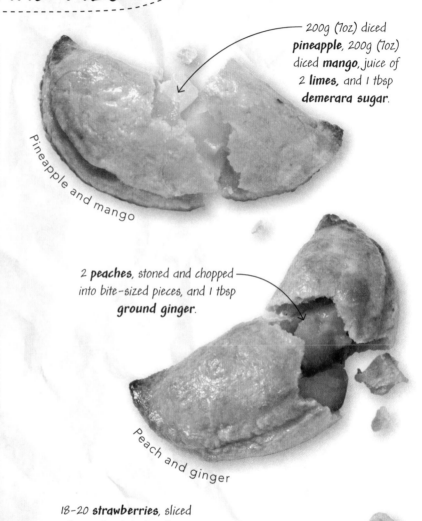

200g (7oz) diced **pineapple**, 200g (7oz) diced **mango**, juice of 2 **limes**, and 1 tbsp **demerara sugar**.

Pineapple and mango

2 **peaches**, stoned and chopped into bite-sized pieces, and 1 tbsp **ground ginger**.

Peach and ginger

18-20 **strawberries**, sliced and tossed with 3 tbsp **honey**.

Strawberries and honey

These neat little pies are a treat at any time of the day and make for the perfect portable snack. Try these delicious fillings or experiment with your own favourite fruity combinations. You could even freeze a batch of the dough and keep it ready for when inspiration strikes!

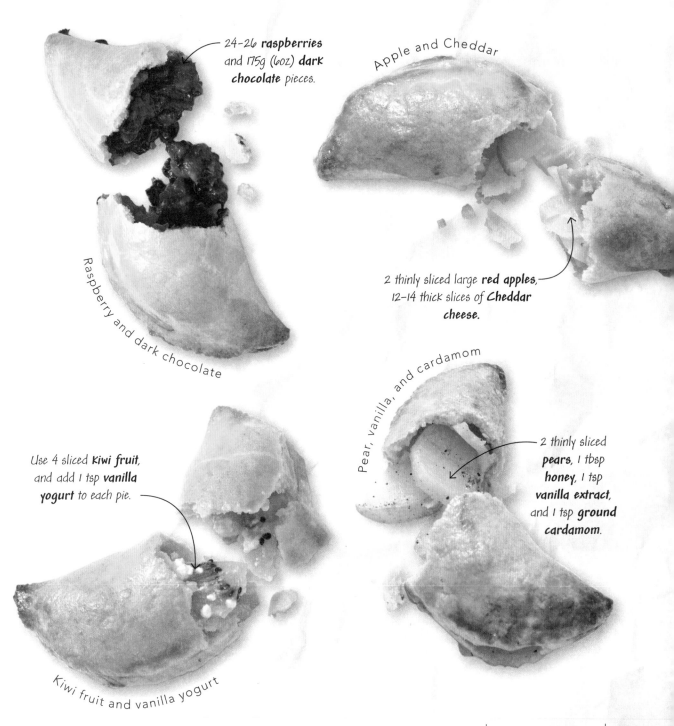

24–26 **raspberries** and 175g (6oz) **dark chocolate** pieces.

Raspberry and dark chocolate

Apple and Cheddar

2 thinly sliced large **red apples**, 12–14 thick slices of **Cheddar cheese.**

Use 4 sliced **kiwi fruit**, and add 1 tsp **vanilla yogurt** to each pie.

Pear, vanilla, and cardamom

2 thinly sliced **pears**, 1 tbsp **honey**, 1 tsp **vanilla extract**, and 1 tsp **ground cardamom.**

Kiwi fruit and vanilla yogurt

EASY BANOFFEE PIE

Using a ready-made tart case is a sneaky way of creating an impressive dessert without having to make your own pastry. You can have a perfect banoffee pie on the table in just 15 minutes!

SERVES 8 • **READY IN** 15 mins

SPECIAL EQUIPMENT Electric hand-held whisk

INGREDIENTS

- 20cm (8in) ready-made tart case
- 200g (7oz) ready-made thick caramel sauce (such as dulce de leche)
- 2–3 ripe bananas
- 300ml (10fl oz) double cream or whipping cream
- 25g (scant 1oz) dark chocolate

① FILL THE TART CASE

Place the tart case on a serving plate. Spoon in the caramel sauce and spread evenly over the bottom. Slice the bananas and scatter over the top.

② WHIP THE CREAM

Place the cream in a bowl and beat with an electric hand whisk until soft peaks form. Spoon the cream over the bananas.

③ ADD CHOCOLATE AND SERVE

Grate the chocolate evenly over the top, and serve.

Why not try different fillings for the tart case? Whipped cream or crème patissière topped with raspberries or sliced strawberries is delicious.

PLAN OF ACTION!
① FILL TART CASE → **②** WHIP CREAM → **③** ADD CHOCOLATE AND SERVE

CHOCOLATE BISCUIT CAKE

Also known as a chocolate fridge cake, this no-bake treat is perfect as a lunchbox nibble. Vary the fruit and nuts to your liking – chopped cherries and hazelnuts work well, for example.

SERVES 6 • **READY IN** 10 mins, plus chilling
SPECIAL EQUIPMENT 20cm (8in) square baking tin

INGREDIENTS

- 150g (5½oz) butter, plus extra for greasing
- 250g (9oz) dark chocolate, broken into pieces
- 2 tbsp golden syrup
- 450g (1lb) digestive biscuits, crushed
- handful of plump golden raisins
- handful of unskinned almonds, roughly chopped

① MELT THE CHOCOLATE MIXTURE

Lightly grease the tin. In a large saucepan, combine the butter, chocolate, and syrup. Cook over a low heat, stirring, until melted and smooth. Remove from the heat.

② ADD THE DRY INGREDIENTS

Stir the biscuits, raisins, and almonds into the chocolate mixture. Mix well, then press the mixture into the tin with the back of a spoon.

③ CHILL, SLICE, AND SERVE

Transfer to the fridge to cool completely. Once the chocolate is set, slice the cake into pieces, and serve.

TIP – To crush the digestive biscuits, put them in a plastic bag and bash with a rolling pin. Don't break them too finely, though – you want the cake to have plenty of texture.

PLAN OF ACTION!   **①** MELT CHOCOLATE MIXTURE → **②** ADD DRY INGREDIENTS → **③** CHILL, SLICE, AND SERVE

CHOCOLATE CHIP COOKIES

These easy-to-make cookies are soft and chewy, and incredibly moreish. Double the recipe if you're feeling greedy or having friends around, then serve with a glass of milk for the perfect afternoon treat!

MAKES 15 • **READY IN** 20 mins, plus cooling

1 CREAM THE BUTTER AND SUGARS

Preheat the oven to 180°C (350°F/Gas 4). In a large bowl, cream together the butter and sugars with an electric hand whisk until light and fluffy. Beat in the egg and vanilla extract.

2 ADD THE FLOUR AND CHOCOLATE CHIPS

Sift together the flour, baking powder, and salt and mix into the wet mixture, until well combined. Finally fold in the chocolate chips.

3 SPOON OUT THE MIX

Place tablespoons of the cookie mixture onto several baking sheets, making sure that they are spaced well apart as they will spread while cooking.

4 BAKE AND COOL

Bake the cookies in the middle of the oven for 13–15 mins, until they are lightly coloured and just cooked. Leave the cookies to cool on the baking sheets for 5 minutes before transferring to a wire rack to cool completely. Serve with a glass of milk.

For lots more quick cookie recipe ideas and variations, see pp240–41.

1		2		3		4
CREAM BUTTER	→	**ADD FLOUR**	→	**SPOON OUT MIX**	→	**BAKE AND COOL**

INGREDIENTS

- - - - - - - - - - - - - - -

100g (3½oz) unsalted butter, softened

100g (3½oz) caster sugar

100g (3½oz) light soft brown sugar

1 large egg

1 tsp vanilla extract

175g (6oz) plain flour

½ tsp baking powder

½ tsp salt

100g (3½oz) milk chocolate chips

COOKIE JAR LUCKY DIP

BUTTERSCOTCH AND MARSHMALLOW COOKIES

Add 100g (3½oz) each of butterscotch chunks and mini marshmallows to the basic dough, then bake.

THUMBPRINT COOKIES

Divide the basic dough into 15 pieces, roll each piece into a ball, flatten it out, and press your thumb into the centre. Fill each "thumbprint" with 1 tsp raspberry jam (or jam of your choice), then bake.

DOUBLE CHOC AND CHERRY COOKIES

Add 4 tbsp cocoa powder, 1 tbsp brown sugar, 100g (3½oz) each of chocolate chunks and dried cherries, and 1 tsp vanilla to the basic dough, then bake.

PEANUT BUTTER COOKIES

Add 4 tbsp peanut butter, 1 tsp vanilla extract, and 50g (1¾oz) crushed peanuts to the basic dough, then bake.

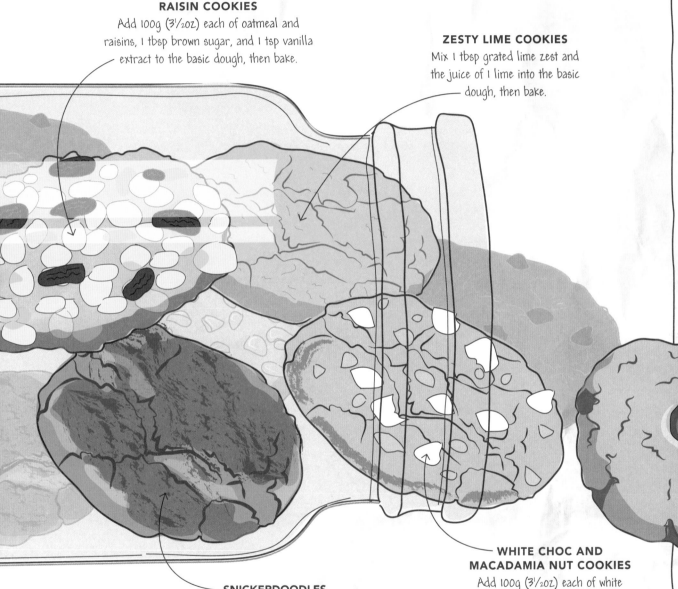

Don't worry if you get caught with your hand in the cookie jar – you deserve a treat, after all! For these scrumptious recipes, follow the basic cookie dough method and baking instructions on pages 238–40 (omitting the chocolate chips), adapt as below, and divide into 15 equal pieces.

OATMEAL AND RAISIN COOKIES
Add 100g (3½oz) each of oatmeal and raisins, 1 tbsp brown sugar, and 1 tsp vanilla extract to the basic dough, then bake.

ZESTY LIME COOKIES
Mix 1 tbsp grated lime zest and the juice of 1 lime into the basic dough, then bake.

WHITE CHOC AND MACADAMIA NUT COOKIES
Add 100g (3½oz) each of white chocolate chunks and chopped macadamia nuts, and 1 tsp vanilla extract to the basic dough, then bake.

SNICKERDOODLES
Mix together 100g (3½oz) sugar, 1 tsp salt, and 2 tbsp ground cinnamon. Divide the basic dough into 15 pieces, roll each piece into a ball, then roll each ball in the sugar and cinnamon mix to coat. Flatten slightly before baking.

QUICK BROWNIES

Soft and moist in the centre and crisp on top, these classic brownies are so easy to prepare. You can store them for up to 3 days in an airtight container.

MAKES 24 • **READY IN** 20–30 mins, plus cooling
SPECIAL EQUIPMENT 23 x 30cm (9 x 12in) brownie tin, or similar

- 175g (6oz) unsalted butter, diced
- 300g (10oz) good-quality dark chocolate, broken into pieces
- 300g (10oz) caster sugar
- 4 large eggs, beaten
- 200g (7oz) plain flour
- 25g (scant 1oz) cocoa powder, plus extra for dusting

MAKE THE BATTER

1 MELT

butter   chocolate   WOODEN SPOON

HEATPROOF BOWL

SAUCEPAN

Melt the butter and chocolate in a bowl over a pan of simmering water. Allow to cool. Preheat the oven to 200°C (400°F/Gas 6).

2 COMBINE

sugar   beaten eggs

Add the sugar and mix well. Then add the eggs, a little at a time, and combine.

3 SIFT AND MIX

flour and cocoa powder   SIEVE

Sift in the flour and cocoa powder. Mix until smooth.

FORM AND BAKE

batter

4 SPREAD

SPATULA

BAKING PARCHMENT

BROWNIE TIN

Line the tin with parchment. Some should hang over the sides. Pour in the batter and spread it out evenly.

Bake for 12–15 minutes, until firm to the touch and a skewer inserted comes out coated with a little batter. Cool completely.

METAL SKEWER

5 BAKE

SLICE AND SERVE

6 SLICE

SHARP KNIFE

hot water

LIFT THE BROWNIE FROM THE TIN AND SCORE THE SURFACE INTO 24 PIECES.

cocoa powder

SIEVE

7 DUST

Slice the brownie along the score lines, wiping the knife and dipping it in hot water between cuts.

Sift cocoa powder over and serve.

SOUR CHERRY AND CHOCOLATE BROWNIES

For a quick yet decadent dessert, try these gooey, fudge-style brownies. The sharp and chewy dried sour cherries contrast wonderfully with the rich, dark chocolate.

MAKES 16 • **READY IN** 20–30 mins, plus cooling
SPECIAL EQUIPMENT 20 x 25cm (8 x 10in) brownie tin or similar

INGREDIENTS

- 150g (5½oz) unsalted butter, diced, plus extra for greasing
- 150g (5½oz) good-quality dark chocolate, broken into pieces
- 250g (9oz) soft light brown muscovado sugar
- 150g (5½oz) self-raising flour, sifted
- 3 eggs
- 1 tsp vanilla extract
- 100g (3½oz) dried sour cherries
- 100g (3½oz) dark chocolate chunks

1 PREPARE THE TIN

Preheat the oven to 200°C (400°F/Gas 6). Grease the brownie tin and line with baking parchment, allowing for some overhang.

2 MAKE THE BATTER

Melt the butter and chocolate in a heatproof bowl over a saucepan of simmering water (make sure the bowl doesn't touch the water as the chocolate may burn). Remove from the heat, add the sugar, and stir to combine. Cool slightly, add the eggs and vanilla extract, and mix to combine. Add the flour and fold it in gently, being careful not to over-mix. Fold in the sour cherries and chocolate chunks.

3 POUR AND BAKE

Pour the batter into the prepared tin and gently spread it out into the corners. Bake in the centre of the oven for 12–15 minutes, or until just firm to the touch and a skewer inserted comes out coated with a little batter.

4 COOL AND STORE

Leave the brownie to cool in the tin for 5 minutes. Then turn out and cut into squares. Place on a wire rack to cool completely, then serve or store for up to 3 days.

 **PLAN OF ACTION!** **1 PREPARE TIN** → **2 MAKE BATTER** → **3 POUR AND BAKE** → **4 COOL AND STORE**

WHITE CHOCOLATE AND MACADAMIA NUT BLONDIES

Blondies are simply white chocolate versions of brownies. The macadamia nuts here add a buttery crunch to these moist treats – a perfect match for the creamy white chocolate.

MAKES 24 • **READY IN** 20–30 mins, plus cooling
SPECIAL EQUIPMENT 20 x 25cm (8 x 10in) brownie tin or similar

INGREDIENTS

- 175g (6oz) unsalted butter, diced, plus extra for greasing
- 300g (10oz) white chocolate, broken into pieces
- 300g (10oz) caster sugar
- 4 large eggs
- 225g (8oz) plain flour, sifted
- 100g (3½oz) macadamia nuts, roughly chopped

1 PREPARE THE TIN

Preheat the oven to 200°C (400°F/ Gas 6). Grease the brownie tin and line with baking parchment, allowing for some overhang.

2 MAKE THE BATTER

Melt the butter and chocolate in a heatproof bowl over a saucepan of simmering water (make sure the bowl doesn't touch the water as the chocolate may burn). Remove, and leave to cool for 20 minutes. Then add the sugar and mix well to combine. Using a balloon whisk, beat in the eggs, one at a time, until well incorporated. Then fold in the flour and stir in the nuts.

3 POUR AND BAKE

Pour the batter into the prepared tin and gently spread it out into the corners. Bake in the centre of the oven for 12–15 minutes, or until just firm to the touch and a skewer inserted comes out coated with a little batter.

4 COOL AND STORE

Leave to cool completely in the tin, then cut into 24 squares and serve or store for up to 5 days.

PLAN OF ACTION! → **1 PREPARE TIN** → **2 MAKE BATTER** → **3 POUR AND BAKE** → **4 COOL AND STORE**

INGREDIENTS

45g (1½oz) butter, softened, plus extra for greasing

250g (9oz) dark chocolate, chopped

115g (4oz) caster sugar

4 eggs

½ tsp pure vanilla extract

45g (1½oz) plain flour

pinch of salt

whipped cream, vanilla ice cream, or hot custard flavoured with orange zest, to serve (optional)

PLAN OF ACTION!

1 PREPARE RAMEKINS → 2 MELT CHOCOLATE → 3 MAKE BATTER

MOLTEN CHOCOLATE PUDDINGS

A treat for all chocoholics, these easy-to-make puddings have a light sponge surrounding a rich, creamy chocolate centre. Add a scoop or two of vanilla ice cream and you've got a simple and speedy decadent dessert.

SERVES 4 • **READY IN** 20 mins
SPECIAL EQUIPMENT 4 x 175ml (6fl oz) ramekins or individual pudding basins

1 PREPARE THE RAMEKINS

Generously butter the sides and bottom of the ramekins. Cut a piece of greaseproof paper to fit in the bottom of each and put in position. Set aside. Preheat the oven to 200°C (400°F/Gas 6).

2 MELT THE CHOCOLATE

Put the chocolate in a heatproof bowl set over a pan of simmering water, without letting the bowl touch the water, and stir for 5 minutes, or until the chocolate is melted and smooth. Set aside.

3 MAKE THE BATTER

While the chocolate is melting, beat the butter and sugar with an electric mixer until blended and smooth. Beat in the eggs one at a time, beating well after each addition, then add the vanilla. Sift the flour and salt together and gently stir in, then stir in the chocolate. Divide the batter equally between the ramekins: the mixture won't fill them to the tops.

4 BAKE THE PUDS

Place the ramekins on a baking tray and bake for 12–15 minutes, or until the sides are set, but the centres are still soft when lightly pressed with your fingertips. Serve the puddings hot, with softly whipped cream, vanilla ice cream, or hot custard flavoured with orange zest, if desired.

TIP – Coarsely chop leftovers and spoon them over vanilla ice cream with hot fudge sauce to make a delicious sundae (see pp220–21 for more sundae ideas).

Try using some of the more exotically flavoured dark chocolate available – such as cardamom and orange, or chilli-flavoured chocolate.

INDEX

Entries in **bold** indicate ingredients.

ACKNOWLEDGMENTS

ABOUT THE AUTHOR

Laura Herring has worked as a writer and cookery editor for some of the UK's top publishers for more than 10 years.

She has worked with many top chefs from around the world on books covering almost every type of cooking from pies to paella to four-tier party cakes. Always in a hurry but never wanting to miss a meal, this is the perfect book for her. She currently lives in London.

ABOUT THE CONTRIBUTOR

Elena Rosemond-Hoerr is the co-author of DK's *The American Cookbook* and contributor to DK's *The Meat Cookbook*. She is a writer, photographer, and author of the award-winning food blog biscuitsandsuch.com. Between developing recipes and writing cookbooks, Elena has a lot of experience fitting quick meals into a busy schedule.

LAURA HERRING WOULD LIKE TO THANK

A huge thank you to everyone who has helped put this beautiful and endlessly useful book together.

To Borra Garson and Louise Leftwich at DML; Peggy Vance, Bob Bridle, and the whole team at DK for their patience in making it all happen and for their expert advice at every step; Harriet Yeomans (star designer!) for making every page look gorgeous; Elena Rosemond-Hoerr for all her creativity. And, of course, my lovely husband, Andy, who is the lucky (and sometimes not-so-lucky) taste-tester in our kitchen!

And to you, the reader: I hope this book puts all the fun back into your quick-cooking adventures.

DK WOULD LIKE TO THANK

Stuart West for new recipe photography; William Reavell for additional photography; Geoff Fennell for photography art direction; Kate Wesson and Jane Lawrie for food styling; Isabel de Cordova for prop styling; Bob Saxton, Kathy Woolley, and Neha Samuel for editorial assistance; Mandy Earey, and Hannah Moore for design assistance; Claire Cross for proofreading; and Vanessa Bird for the index.

All photography and artworks © Dorling Kindersley
For further information see: **www.dkimages.com**